Advance Praise for *Afternoons with Harper Lee*

"No biography of any person has made me feel so palpably that I sat with its subject as Wayne Flynt's *Afternoons with Harper Lee*. NewSouth Books has given us a seat next to one of the most important writers, globally, of the last hundred years. Flynt's contextualizing of his (and our) visits with important information about both local and national time and place completes the experience."

— **Sena Jeter Naslund, author of *Four Spirits,**
***Ahab's Wife*, and others**

"Wayne Flynt's prose flows as gracefully as the rivers of Alabama, clear and lyrical, in this special volume, in which a portrait of Harper Lee—variously vulnerable and strong-willed in her privacy—emerges. *Afternoons with Harper Lee* is a captivating remembrance of an unlikely but deep friendship borne of great storytelling."

— **Patti Callahan Henry, *New York Times*-**
bestselling author of *Becoming Mrs. Lewis*

"Wayne Flynt is the great Talmudic scholar of Alabama, and this vivid, affecting deconstruction of his friendship with Harper Lee through the history that produced them both is a huge reward and pleasure for those of us who understand that, unaccountably, all roads seem to lead to our grand and terrifying state."

— **Diane McWhorter, author of *Carry Me Home:***
Birmingham, Alabama—The Climactic Battle
of the Civil Rights Revolution

"Many people have written books about Harper Lee. Wayne Flynt knew her better than any of them. This is a fond and very personal portrait, full of stories and laughter. The lady's unique astringent voice comes through loud and clear. Nelle Harper Lee would have loved this book, and so do I."
   — **Mark Childress, author of** *Crazy in Alabama* **and** *Georgia Bottoms*

"*Afternoons with Harper Lee* is a celebration of friendship, literature, and how place and history shape us all. It's full of wisdom, love, and loss—heartbreaking and heart-healing in equal measure. I so enjoyed this book!"
   — **Daniel Wallace, author of** *Big Fish*

"Often described as reclusive, Nelle Harper Lee was warm and genial with close friends such as Southern historian Wayne Flynt. Based on a decade of delightful conversations and shared storytelling in the Southern tradition, *Afternoons with Harper Lee* reveals the multi-faceted personality—witty, caustic, generous, self-deprecating, kind, searingly honest—of one of our nation's most revered writers."
   — **Cynthia Tucker, Pulitzer-winning columnist and coauthor of** *The Southernization of America*

"Though Nelle's world became much smaller in her later years, the stories told here reveal much about the wit, insight, and powers of description and self-deprecation which defined her to the end. Thanks for giving us such an admirable portrait of this great, complicated, and most famous writer."
   — **Paul Dewey, Nelle Harper Lee friend and correspondent, son of** *In Cold Blood*'s **Al Dewey**

Afternoons
with
Harper Lee

AFTERNOONS WITH HARPER LEE

Wayne Flynt

NewSouth Books

AN IMPRINT OF
The University of Georgia Press
Athens

NSB

Published by NewSouth Books
an imprint of the University of Georgia Press
Athens, Georgia 30602
www.ugapress.org/imprints/newsouth-books

Most NewSouth/University of Georgia Press titles
are available from popular ebook vendors.

Printed in the United States of America
22 23 24 25 26 C 5 4 3 2 1

Library of Congress Control Number: 2022943692
ISBN 9781588384874 (hardback : alk. paper)
ISBN 9781588384881 (ebook)

In memory of

Dorothy ("Dartie") Flynt

and Nelle Harper Lee

Contents

Preface

Nelle Harper Lee and Dartie Flynt could have been sisters. Nelle was born in 1926, Dartie twelve years later. There was less age difference between them than between Nelle and her sister Alice.

Both their fathers were pious, godly men, generous in expressions of love and slow to anger or to judge others. When discipline was required, they were inclined toward gentle reprimands rather than physical punishment. Their fathers imprinted them more than their mothers.

Dartie and Nelle were intensely private, preferring the company of family and close friends to that of others. Both loved literature, especially fiction. Dartie taught middle and high school English and preferred Russian writers, especially Leo Tolstoy, Boris Pasternak, and Aleksandr Solzhenitsyn. Danish writer Isak Dinesen and J. R. R. Tolkien also enthralled her. Nelle preferred Jane Austen but read across many nationalities.

Both loved theater, especially Shakespeare. Dartie persuaded me to purchase season tickets to the Alabama Shakespeare Festival for half a century, and Nelle watched her last (and favorite) play, *King Lear*, with us.

At Samford University where we met, Dartie was a Speech/

Theater/English major, and, like Nelle, a wordsmith. I discovered that the hard way when I asked her to edit drafts of my first book. Perhaps she was getting even with me for a life then filled with cooking, house cleaning, and changing diapers while I was teaching the most intellectually challenging students of my forty-year career. Whatever her motive, I will never forget her first criticism of my manuscript: "What do you mean in this paragraph?" I churlishly replied: "Just what I said!" She stood, walked away, and fired a retreating salvo over her shoulder: "Well, the words don't convey what you intended to say!" I reread the paragraph half a dozen times before making the revision she suggested and apologizing.

Because of Dartie's lifetime of writing scripts, performing oral interpretations of literature, and narrating church pageants, she understood what J. K. Rowling put in the mind of Professor Dumbledore: "Words are, in my not so humble opinion, our most inexhaustible source of magic." And exact words are better than proximate words. I always knew what I wanted to say, but I could be much too casual in how I put words on paper.

When it came to recalling Nelle's exact words, phrases, colloquialisms, voice inflections, facial expressions, even hesitations, pauses, or gaps in conversation, Dartie was many times my master. She often corrected our journals, telling me, "You have accurately recorded what she meant but not what she said."

More importantly, she was the one who initially attracted Nelle's affection, not because of any effort on her part but because when we first became friends Nelle had just suffered a stroke, and Dartie was in her fifteenth year of the Parkinson's disease that would take her life nearly three years to the day after Nelle died.

As Nelle was learning how to operate her wheelchair, Dartie was trying to walk with a cane or walker, but often falling. Confined to a wheelchair and having just suffered a torn rotator cuff in a fall, one day Nelle exasperatedly told Dartie: "I hope this never happens to you!" Unfortunately, it did.

Both women remained intellectually alert despite their physical limitations. Both were incredibly courageous. Both battled depression without succumbing to it. In a sense, they held each other up. Each enjoyed wordplay at my expense.

In one way they differed. Nelle preferred frumpy clothes, especially pedal pushers and T-shirts, and wore no makeup. Dartie dressed to the nines for every occasion and particularly favored spiffy hats, many of them vintage survivors from the 1920s and 1930s. Nelle was frump. Dartie was style.

Although I wrote this book absent my soulmate for nearly sixty years, she is present in spirit and on every page, a true co-author in every sense save one: the book would have profited from her criticism and revisions. As Nelle correctly observed one afternoon, "You are a single entity with two separate parts."

WHAT WE OFFER THE world is not a biography, although it contains the essence of the form. Some biographies tell about a person without telling what the person is about. One conveys facts. Another uses anecdotes and stories to convey the meaning of facts. Richard Holmes, one of Britain's best practitioners of the art, wrote that the biographer's "most valuable but perilous weapon" is empathy. Writing about another human being is "a simple act of complicated friendship" which employs knowledge and understanding in order to render a life.

Readers who anticipated an *exposé* or a tell-all biography resulting from our sixty-four afternoons with Harper Lee will be disappointed. We never pried into her private life, although she occasionally revealed traces of it. We were simply friends who shared similar interests in a time when she needed someone to visit often and help her pass lonely afternoons. We came to love her sufficiently to allow her to depart this world as she lived in it: as a free spirit; a mystery; author of America's most beloved novel; as one of the most remarkable women of the twentieth century.

As we understood the relationship, we were merely three Alabamians spending afternoons slipping the bonds of small-town Auburn and Monroeville for the cosmos beyond of literature, history, and friendship. Our friendship deepened after her 2007 stroke, and "Harper" became "Nelle" at her request.

Laozi's famous proverb in the *Tao Te Ching (Dao De Jing)* that a journey of a thousand miles begins with a single step could not be a better metaphor for our friendship with Alice, Louise, and Nelle Lee. Serendipity, or something even less ostentatious such as luck, was involved. Almost nothing was planned. Events and conversations meandered and just happened. As a result, I have framed the book like the friendship—not a linear account of Nelle's life, but like a ten-year-long conversation weaving in and out of chronological order. I refer to "afternoons" in the title for reasons of geographical reality. Until I retired in 2005 from teaching, the only times available to us for visits were Sunday afternoons. The round trip from Auburn to Eufaula where Louise Lee Conner lived took two hours. Monroeville, where Alice practiced law and Nelle lived following her stroke, required five hours round trip. Trips both ways from Auburn to Birmingham where Nelle spent six months in physical rehabilitation consumed four hours. We planned our Monroeville visits with Nelle and Alice for afternoons following lunch, and in Eufaula we transported Louise Conner to her favorite café before an afternoon of bird-watching and storytelling.

Before the Lee–Flynt visits ended, we had traveled many thousands of miles on asphalt, and much further in memory and imagination. Dartie and Nelle made the journey possible.

Acknowledgments

I believe that one characteristic of friendship is the willingness to interrupt a busy life in order to save a friend from errors. All those I acknowledge spent many days on this journey with me, challenging and correcting. Either a list of people who helped with this book will be longer than the book itself or incomplete. Nevertheless, some deserve special recognition.

Obviously, four people now gone—Dartie Flynt, Louise Lee Conner, Alice Lee, and Nelle Harper Lee—were the major actors. Hank and Ed Conner played significant supporting roles.

"The Usual Suspects," especially Susan Doss and Cathy Randall, were more than bit players but were infrequently on center stage. Cammie Plummer East Cowan furnished many of the best anecdotes about Nelle and her Mobile circle of friends.

New York philanthropist George Landegger flew me to New York to conduct interviews and underwrites the Harper Lee and Eugene Garcia Literary Scholar awards. Alabama Supreme Court Associate Justice Gorman Houston shared his manuscript about Nelle. Paul Dewey—son of Alvin and Marie and now a retired

Oregon attorney—provided numerous stories about Nelle and Truman Capote in Kansas.

My Auburn University at Montgomery colleague, Nancy Anderson, offered her encyclopedic knowledge and a significant collection of obscure published sources about Nelle. When I served as founding general editor of the online *Encyclopedia of Alabama*, I persuaded Nancy to write an essay about Harper Lee, which quickly became one of its most popular worldwide, receiving millions of "hits." Anyone who can shove football coach Paul "Bear" Bryant down the list of most popular Alabamians globally deserves respect if not adulation.

Tonja Carter, now senior partner at A. C. and Alice Lee's law firm, played a major role in the final stage of Nelle's life. Tonja, with Ed Conner and Hank Conner, Louise's two sons, were stalwart protectors of Nelle's personal privacy. No one could have been more faithful. I never asked any of them personal questions that only they and their Monroeville cousin Edwin Lee could have answered. My curiosity about Nelle never tempted me to violate their family honor. Rest in peace, Nelle—they did good. Ed Conner read the manuscript for family mistakes, expending an enormous amount of time and earning my everlasting gratitude.

Yvonne Williams—retired English teacher, tactful corrector of my spelling and overly long sentences, and member of the Pilgrims Sunday School class that I teach—typed this manuscript accurately, as she always does. Despite delivery of a manuscript written by hand and containing far too many arrows, margin notes, and passages that appear to be written in another language, she persevered to the end.

My sons Sean and David carefully read and critiqued the

manuscript as well. Both are gifted writers in their own spheres. More importantly, they have grudges to settle with their old man from childhood and are gleefully willing to point out his flaws.

Only Dartie had more potential grievances which might have scuttled the entire project. Her eternally private spirit warned me away when I was tempted to tell more about Nelle than anyone has a right to know. Part of her persona, Dartie insisted, as for all women, was mystery. Leave it at that.

Thanks to them all.

Afternoons
with
Harper Lee

Chapter 1

Southern Friends and Families

THE LEES. IN THE SOUTH, MOST PEOPLE ESTABLISH INDIVIDUAL identity through family connections. If they can't find a blood relation match, they search for similarities of town, state, university, church, occupation, or even for people with the same football allegiance, hobby, or preference for pork barbecue rather than beef brisket.

Southerners are also more likely to stay put, especially since the "Great Migration" to the North by African Americans between 1917 and 1970. Notwithstanding waves of out-migration of both blacks and whites, prompted by severe economic hardship, Southerners have a strong attachment to home. Loyalty to a place or family is often stronger than even the allure of fame and fortune.

Nelle Harper Lee was an exception to this pattern although she was born into it. Her life began in the small county seat town of Monroeville in Monroe County in southwest Alabama on April 28, 1926. Officially, Monroe is part of the fabled Alabama Black Belt, so called because of its rich, dark topsoil atop deep chalk formations created by tiny creatures that decomposed in a sea that once covered Alabama as far north as the Appalachian foothills. When the topsoil is wet, it changes color to a grayish-black.

Geologists who study soil types find only a narrow band of such earth in northern Monroe County. But it was sufficient to make the county a major producer of cotton, unlike counties to the south and east.

Southwest Alabama was also easy to reach. One-tenth of all water coursing through the lower forty-eight states flows through Alabama, most of it north to south before emptying into Mobile Bay. Early settlement converged on Mobile from explorers moving west out of Spanish Florida or east from French Louisiana.

Monroe and Mobile counties were the most populous in the southwest corner of the state, with most of Monroe's population living near the broad Alabama River which split the Black Belt. The variety of soil types and crops mirrored the Black Belt and also determined the distribution of African Americans. In 1860, they constituted a slight majority, accounting for the county's success growing cotton and majority white vote in favor of secession from the Union.

North of Monroe, Black Belt counties stretched all the way across the state, from Eufaula on the Chattahoochee River, which separates Alabama and Georgia, to Demopolis on the Tombigbee, near the state's border with Mississippi. In the 1860 census, the Black Belt constituted part of a vast cotton kingdom beginning in central South Carolina and continuing into East Texas, accounting for 40 percent of U.S. exports and 20 percent of the country's gross domestic product. For whites who lived there, it was the richest place on earth. For its slave laborers, it was the most oppressive place on earth.

Black Belt wealth promoted education for the few, frequently conducted by private tutors in plantation schools, which was how

Nelle Lee's mother was educated at the Finch plantation on a bluff overlooking the Alabama River. Such families emphasized art, literature, music, theater, and acquisition of substantial private libraries. Frances Finch Lee was a classical pianist and a graduate of the state's women's college at a time when most white Alabama women did not complete even secondary school.

LOUISE LEE CONNER's SON, Ed, remembered that both his Finch grandmother and his great-aunt Alice Marshall Finch were sent downriver to a "finishing school" in Mobile where they learned to play the piano and "sew a fine seam." Mobile, some sixty miles south of Monroeville, was the unofficial capital of southwest Alabama and rivaled New Orleans for dominance of the Gulf Coast in both commerce and culture. Mobile boasted the nation's oldest Mardi Gras festival and a cosmopolitan population which contributed both to its erudition and its hedonism. The city's Spring Hill College was the South's oldest Jesuit institution of higher learning and was also Alabama's first college of any kind. The city's Catholic population was also the state's largest. Mobile also contained a small but influential Jewish population that competed successfully in mercantile and professional life and sustained a high level of Jewish religious identity. The Lee family patronized one of the Jewish department stores owned by the Reiss family and relied on the city's doctors and hospitals for serious medical procedures.

More importantly so far as Nelle was concerned, Mobile produced Alabama's finest literary heritage. Augusta Evans Wilson became the first American woman to earn a hundred thousand dollars in royalties. Her novel *St. Elmo* was published just after the Civil War, sold millions of copies, and has never been out of print. One generation later, William March, a gay man from a prominent local family and a veteran of fierce fighting during the First World War, wrote *Company K*, which critics consider one of America's finest anti-war novels. Yet another generation into the future, African American novelist, essayist, and Mobile native Albert Murray captured the jazz dissonance of southwest Alabama during a distinguished literary career, most notably in his memoir *South to a Very Old Place*. Harvard University naturalist E. O. Wilson, who grew up in the city, won two Pulitzer Prizes.

ALTHOUGH UNIQUE IN ITS own way, Monroe County boasted few distinctions. Monroeville was no Mobile when Nelle Lee departed Alabama in 1949 at age twenty-three, or when a stroke and partial paralysis compelled her to return in 2007 at age eighty-one. Monroe County was among twenty-two original Alabama counties at statehood in 1819 and was named for President James Monroe. The southern part of the county was part of Alabama's coastal plain that stretched to the Gulf of Mexico. Hurricanes and tropical storms dumped more than fifty inches of rain annually on soil which, though sandier than the Black Belt, could still produce bountiful harvests. Mobile novelist Charles McNair described the region as "sinfully lush. Anything grows. You get the idea that dogs even bury bones with high hopes."

Immediately south of Monroe County, the Mobile/Alabama River overspreads the land creating a delta of swamps resplendent with giant cypress trees and populated with alligators, bear, deer, and birds migrating between Canada and Mexico. Many Alabama rivers empty into this estuary and thence into Mobile Bay and the Gulf of Mexico.

No one knew this history better than Alice Lee, the oldest of the three sisters. Universally and reverentially referred to as "Miss Alice," she was the most respected custodian of local history. I do not recall mentioning a book about southwest Alabama that she had not read. She was also the Lee/Finch family historian. She had a habit of reading four books at a time, with one in the living room, another in the kitchen, a third in the bedroom, and the fourth at her law office to read during her lunch break. Although Alice had a large library of what the sisters called "scientific history," including my books, she also appreciated "romance and adventure." And why not? If romance and adventure was your thing, you could hardly do better than live in southwest Alabama.

Take the place names. As part of our informal "education," she explained that Murder Creek on the eastern edge of the county memorialized a company of pioneers who had been massacred on their way to Louisiana in 1788. They were camped beside the creek when a white man nicknamed "Cat," a black man named Bob, and a Hilibi Indian nicknamed "the Man-Slayer" slaughtered them. Bob and "Man-Slayer" escaped, but "Cat" was caught and hanged. Alice told me the story as adventure. I processed the story as "scientific history," the earliest account I knew of Alabama biracial crime.

Burnt Corn Creek to the east of Murder Creek began at a spring where two mixed-race men had stopped when one became sick. The other cooked corn for him before departing, and those who found the charred grain named the spring Burnt Corn. It was near the Federal Road (though "path" would be a more appropriate designation in the early days), the major route from Georgia to New Orleans and the Louisiana Territory. Where Wolf Trail intersected the road, 150 white militiamen ambushed a faction of Creek warriors called "Red Sticks" on July 27, 1813, as they returned from the British port of Pensacola with arms and ammunition. The Red Sticks fled into the cane break, where they regrouped and counterattacked, routing the undisciplined white soldiers.

During the ensuing war, Red Sticks plundered and burned isolated farms and cabins in the Tombigbee settlements in southwest Alabama. Whites fled to hastily constructed fortifications such as Fort Mims at the juncture of Monroe, Baldwin, and Mobile counties. Some 250 white men, women, and children together with friendly Creeks sought refuge in the fort, which was defended by poorly trained militiamen. They were no match for Red Stick warriors who overran the fort on August 30, 1813. Historian Albert Pickett's colorful account of the ensuing massacre, collected from survivors, was filled with gory details: two hundred scalps; hundreds of painted war clubs, each signifying a corpse found in the fort. Half the Red Stick warriors were killed or wounded as well. The massacre at Fort Mims was the largest Indian victory in North America since South Carolina's Yamassee War in 1715.

The only story by Alice rivaling the Fort Mims massacre concerned a famous canoe fight some forty miles upriver from her ancestral home at Finch's Landing. E. S. Liles, who attended school in Mobile for three weeks before dropping out and eventually becoming a contractor, was my source for the story. Before his storytelling father's death in 1941, Liles recorded the family's version of how Jim Smith, his great-uncle, had helped two white adventurers named Sam Dale and Jerry Austell and a black man named Caesar kill eleven Red Sticks traveling downriver on a log raft. According to the story, the four were finishing a meal of raccoon meat prepared by Caesar on the banks of the Alabama River when they spied a log raft held together with grape vines floating past. Caesar volunteered his canoe, hewn from a log, for the chase. The faster canoe quickly overtook the raft, and Caesar hooked his leg across the canoe and onto the raft. In the ensuing battle with axes, knives, and rifles—fired once then used as clubs—the attackers dispatched the raft-load of Red Sticks, all of whom were killed or swam for their lives in the swift current.

To both Liles and Alice, storytelling was a mental exercise in the power of memory and imagination, with details confused between the two. Oftentimes fiction intrudes on facts, filtering real-life events through romance and adventure. That makes for great storytelling but not necessarily reliable history. Or, as Nelle once scolded me, the difference between novelists and historians is that novelists "don't allow facts to ruin a good story."

HAVING GROWN UP LISTENING to such stories, Nelle's description of her Monroe County lineage was no surprise. Simon Finch, her maternal ancestor from the hauntingly beautiful Cornwall region of England, was a fur-trapping Methodist dissenter from the Anglican Church who migrated to Mobile for both economic and religious reasons. In time, he traveled upriver, acquired land, and began growing cotton at Finch's Landing. Alice explained that her Finch grandfather probably was bequeathed a slave in Virginia, but never learned about the will. Her other great-great-grandfathers owned substantial land in the county. One farmed a plantation with thirty-nine slaves, the other with even more. Following a characteristic American story of generational upward mobility, her Finch ancestors became economically prosperous and secure if not opulently wealthy, living in a multi-story plantation house by the twentieth century.

In addition to borrowing freely from family stories about the Finches, Nelle seemed fascinated by the thinly populated Red Hills just north of Finch's Landing. Given her curiosity about the mysterious and criminal, strange people and even stranger places, the Red Hills would have been a case of deep calling to deep.

Where the Black Belt sharply descends into the relatively flat coastal plain, the Red Hills constitute a geological aberration, a place of waterfalls where they are not supposed to exist, and surprising flora and fauna. Barely a month after Nelle's death, her Mobile friend E. O. Wilson received the annual Harper Lee Award recognizing Alabama's Distinguished Writer of the Year. While accepting the prize, the famed Harvard University naturalist recalled Harper's fascination with the mysterious Red Hills. Wilson explained why. The Red Hills are not only home to twenty-four types of oak trees, probably the world's largest concentration of diverse oak species, but also to the giant nocturnal Red Hills salamander found nowhere else on earth.

The Red Hills were thinly populated by fiercely proud settlers who preferred privacy to prosperity. They eked out a subsistence living by trapping animals and growing what their families consumed on small plots of cleared land. During prosperous times they made a little money selling surplus crops or moonshine whiskey in Monroeville. During hard times, they lost their land to bank foreclosures or entitlement, legal transfer of land ownership at death or departure. I concluded that this seemed the most likely habitation for the fictional world of the Cunninghams in *To Kill a Mockingbird*, and the site of "Old Sarum."

History as romance and adventure served a useful purpose in the Lee family because Monroe County never had a golden age. In 1930, when Nelle Lee was four years old, the county's population peaked at 30,000. During the 1940s, it declined by 13 percent, two of its expatriates being Truman Capote and Nelle Harper Lee. Monroeville's population was 1,300 when Nelle was born in 1926; 2,700 when she left for New York City in 1949; 6,500 when she returned in 2007; and 6,070 when she died in 2016.

Whatever the decade, two polar opposites defined Monroeville: the town was a phenomenal incubator of successful writers, and it was the county seat of racial injustice. Between 1900 and the writing of *Mockingbird*, the county lynched an estimated dozen or more black men. The fate of Tom Robinson in *Mockingbird* is loosely based on a real case of racial injustice which involved Harper's father's vain attempt to persuade a black man to plead guilty to a crime he did not commit in order to avoid the death penalty.

In 1989 a trial judge nearly reprised history. Black resident Walter McMillian was wrongfully convicted of murdering a young white woman. Virtually all evidence except the testimony of an addled white ne'er-do-well—who constantly contradicted himself—acquitted the hard-working McMillian, whose actual offense to community norms was a consensual sexual relationship with a much younger, married white woman. The conflicted jury found McMillian guilty of murder but was sufficiently dubious of the state's "star" witness to hand down a sentence of life in prison rather than the death penalty. The trial judge overrode the jury's recommendation.

McMillian languished on death row for six years before Bryan Stevenson, a young attorney working in Montgomery, reopened the case. The ensuing story, related in Stevenson's memoir and subsequent movie, *Just Mercy*, triggered a racial soul-searching not only in Alabama, but nationwide in the aftermath of the killing of George Floyd in Minneapolis. Stevenson's Equal Justice Initiative nonprofit legal group and its acclaimed National Memorial for Peace and Justice made the author into an African American version of Atticus Finch, minus the fictional hero's racial baggage.

Such black–white racial drama could have played out in any Alabama county during the era of apartheid, or for that matter, in Indiana, which had the highest Ku Klux Klan membership in the nation during the 1920s, or in Oregon, which enacted Klan-sponsored legislation. When four-term Alabama Governor George C. Wallace campaigned for the Democratic presidential nomination in Wisconsin, Michigan, and Maryland in 1968 and 1972, boisterous crowds of whites supported him as emotionally in Milwaukee, Flint, Detroit, and on the Eastern Shore as in Alabama. But perhaps no Alabama family privately expressed more contempt for Wallace's opportunistic racial demagoguery than Monroeville's Lee family.

THE FLYNTS. As NORTH Alabama natives, Dartie and I initially considered the Lees to be from a strange and different world. In some sense, they were. Given our many differences, our decades-long friendship could be considered an anomaly or even a miracle. My Calhoun County ancestors in the Appalachian foothills of northeastern Alabama shared nothing with the Lees except a river. My grandfather was a sharecropper on bottomland near the Coosa River, which flowed into the Alabama, thence through Monroe County to Mobile. There was not a lawyer in the Flynt family, and I was a first-generation college graduate. Dartie graduated from Gadsden High School, thirty miles north of my Anniston High School, two years before I graduated. Many events I describe in this book happened in East Central Alabama counties from Etowah (Gadsden), Calhoun (Anniston), Clay (Ashland), Tallapoosa (Alexander City), to Barbour (Eufaula) and Dale (Ozark).

Despite Harper Lee's empathetic writing in *Mockingbird* about "Scout" Finch's protective inclinations toward Walter Cunningham and his downwardly mobile family, she understood little of the grievances of poor white sharecroppers and marginalized people. Furthermore, her father was a state legislator who helped perpetuate voter suppression by way of poll taxes and literacy tests, both of which disenfranchised my illiterate grandfather. Dartie's people were flushed off the poor mountainous land of Clay County into the new textile mills of Sylacauga a few miles away.

Another strike against us was that Dartie's father and brother were Baptist preachers, as was I in another life. Baptists were as much the imperial denomination of North Alabama as Methodism was of the more affluent Black Belt. My ministerial career ended precipitously when I read too literally the twenty-fifth chapter of Matthew's Gospel where the apostle wrote that no matter how much one believes in Jesus, heaven doesn't admit people who refuse to feed the hungry, give water to the thirsty, care for widows and orphans, visit the sick and imprisoned, or welcome strangers into the land. I continued preaching that gospel until I realized how few white evangelicals believed it. Dartie, the daughter and sister of kind-hearted Baptist ministers, did not strengthen our case with Nelle, who considered "kind-hearted Baptists" to be an oxymoron.

So far as a sense of shared identity was involved, Nelle was no fan of Baptists, Auburn University, or the state of Alabama in general. She was also highly suspicious of academic friends of her sisters, convinced that such people had little genuine interest in *them* and were primarily focused on learning about *her*.

Although Dartie and I had read *Mockingbird* while in graduate school in the early 1960s and were proud of the author's Alabama origins, we had never sought to contact her or her sisters. In fact, the more we read about her, the more reclusive she seemed. During our decade of close friendship, we changed our minds about that. She, like Dartie, was intensely private and took her time to cultivate friendships, but she was not reclusive. She moved to New York City because it was the perfect choice for an aspiring writer who was an intensely private person. As she discovered after returning to Monroeville to live the last decade of her life, partially paralyzed, Alabamians may be willing to give you the shirts off their backs, but in the process they often meddle in your life.

Early in my teaching career, we had no more time for her than she for us. I taught heavy class loads at Samford University in Birmingham, my alma mater, meaning that Dartie had to raise two sons virtually alone, plus sewing her own clothes, cooking, and cleaning house, buried as deeply in her domestic sphere as I was in my academic one.

As years passed and I left Samford for Auburn University, my class load declined to near normal for professors, and the boys grew up. Dartie and I became reacquainted, began to read fiction again, and traveled together.

ONE TRIP IN 1983 took us to Eufaula, one of the most beautiful and interesting Black Belt towns, for an Auburn University-sponsored "History and Heritage" festival. The small city not only anchored the eastern edge of the Black Belt to Georgia across the Chattahoochee River but was also located in Barbour County, which has produced more Alabama governors than any other, including four-term governor George C. Wallace.

The festival planning committee included Nelle's sister, Louise, who had attended Auburn University where she met her future husband, Hershel "Hank" Conner. He became a successful businessman and Auburn trustee, and she was a respected civic volunteer. Now widowed, she knew that Nelle despised public speaking in general and events like ours in particular.

As one of two historians on the planning committee, my second choice for keynote speaker was Truman Capote. If we could not have Harper Lee, then why not her childhood friend who also had Alabama connections? Of course, I did not know about their estrangement or that his addiction to alcohol and drugs meant he might agree to speak but arrive in a drunken stupor, as likely to fall off the stage as to complete a rambling, incoherent presentation.

Louise Conner did know all this and begged her sister to save the committee and community from humiliation by speaking herself. Nelle's consent to do something she so despised was the best evidence of Lee family solidarity and affection.

Nelle's fascinating lecture was unrelated to her novel, New York's literati, Truman Capote, or literature in general. She chose a subject dear to the family, "Romance and Adventure in Alabama History," centered on the career of Albert James Pickett—Montgomery cotton planter, slave owner, and historian, who spent seventeen years gathering firsthand accounts from the state's pioneering white settlers to write and publish in 1851 the first history of Alabama. I learned that Pickett was the source of many of Alice's stories about southwest Alabama.

Faithful to the theme of a "history and heritage" conference, Nelle strayed far afield from fiction, which only amplified her anxiety. We learned decades later during afternoon conversations that public speaking terrified her. In the run-up to such appearances, anxiety attacks made her physically ill. To calm her nerves, she fortified herself with a few drinks.

Our friend and Auburn University at Montgomery professor Nancy Anderson—who was one of the nation's most meticulous Harper Lee scholars and whom I would later recruit to write the Lee essay for the online *Encyclopedia of Alabama*—was a program personality that Saturday in Eufaula. As they waited nervously backstage for introductions to end, Nancy timidly introduced herself to Nelle. The famous novelist exclaimed in panic: "Are you as terrified as I am? I let my sister talk me into this, and I feel like an owl out in daylight. Never again!"

Nelle's premise in her presentation, although true and inspiring, was also ahistorical: History written with passion and romance by a person who had lived through the times he described could excite emotions of love and sacrifice seemingly beyond the power of more recent historians. Her conclusion expressed the Lee family vision of history:

> Pickett's *History of Alabama*, this unique treasure now lies hidden in the old family bookcases, has been discarded by libraries, sometimes turns up in rummage sales, and is certainly not used in our schools. In my opinion it should be in every high school library in the state.
>
> I have no idea what today's historians think of Albert Pickett—very little, I should guess, for Pickett's history is composed of small dramas within a huge drama, much of it drawn from memories of those who were there, from individuals whose bravery and sacrifice created the state of Alabama. Modern research techniques and professional objective evaluations were unknown to Pickett as they were unknown to his contemporaries Macaulay and Prescott, but then who reads them anymore?

Nelle left that rhetorical question dangling in the springtime mugginess of the high school auditorium packed with people who did not care what Harper Lee thought of Albert Pickett, whom most of them had never heard of. They had come so they could tell their grandchildren they had once heard her speak, met her, shook her hand.

I felt as though Lee had spent the evening trashing more than a century of "scientific history," including mine. As she proudly brandished her favorite nineteenth-century historians—Thomas Babington (Lord) Macaulay of England, and American William Prescott, who wrote about Spain and Latin America—I grew more anxious. Whether from heat generated by the warm weather and packed auditorium or heat from her assault on "scientific history" such as I wrote, I felt a little woozy. I vaguely remember Dartie taking my hand and asking if I was all right as I shifted uneasily in my seat.

Exhausted as Nelle was by the excruciating ordeal, she consented to sign copies of *Mockingbird*. After she autographed our son Sean's copy, I handed her our copy to sign. She dismissed me with a flippant, "I only sign books for children!" I remember wondering whether someone had revealed to her that I was not only an adult but also one of those villainous "scientific historians" who had ripped the romance and adventure from the pages of Alabama history books. I didn't think quickly enough to ask if she realized that one of her idols, William Prescott, was considered to be America's first "scientific historian."

To be truthful, although I valued Albert Pickett's preservation of the earliest accounts of the state's history and had taught a course in oral history using some of his interview techniques, I did not relish his celebration of Alabama's cotton kingdom, slavery, or the grandeur of the world they bequeathed us. Despite my disagreements with Alice and Nelle about our understanding of history and how to write it, we shared a common affection both for history as storytelling and for telling Alabama's story.

They, like us, also enjoyed tracing history through their own family, although the Lees' family narrative was much different from ours. Because Lee women were long-lived—Alice died at age 103, Louise at 93, Nelle two months short of 90—they were half as old as the state and remembered a lot.

Their evolving views on race, pioneering forays into the legal profession and American literature, and fierce independence, represented quite a departure from their Confederate grandfather's world. If there had been a category that began "First Alabama woman to . . .," Alice's name would probably have ended the sentence. She was one of the first female attorneys in southwest Alabama, the first woman to lead the Alabama-West Florida Methodist Conference, the oldest woman practicing law in the United States at age one hundred. Monroeville's Kiwanis Club awarded her its first "Citizen of the Year" honor despite the fact that the club did not (yet) accept women members.

One of the finest aspects of our decade-long friendship with Nelle Harper Lee was that it came as a package deal including her two sisters. Before Nelle's stroke in 2007 and return to Alabama, we had treasured a two-decade friendship with Alice and Louise. During those years, we lived contentedly in Alabama, and Nelle was equally satisfied in New York City. Our only contact with her after the Eufaula festival was her letter chiding me for an op-ed column in which I misidentified Louise Lee Conner as the youngest Lee sister. I was later tempted to remind her how easy it is to confuse ages when she constantly referred to us as "kiddos," as if we were a part of different generations, when only twelve years separated Dartie and Nelle, and fourteen separated us. But I apologized without mentioning my unease with her philosophy of history.

Except for a serendipitous invitation from Alice to speak at a Methodist women's conference about the Bible, poverty, and social justice, our lives never would have intersected again. In such lectures, I frequently cited *Mockingbird* as a story about devout Christians who occasionally transcended their secular cultures to embrace the teachings of Christ. Louise, by then a widow, attended the conference, as did Dartie. When the event ended, Louise invited us to visit "sometime." Knowing that by Alabama social conventions "Come see me sometime" might or might not convey serious intent, I responded: "Mrs. Conner, do you *really* want us to visit you, or are you just talking Southern?" Both sisters laughed, and Louise said, "Yes, I would like that!" with a trace of genuine loneliness.

Louise was ten when Nelle was born and often watched after her and Truman Capote. She attended the county-wide white high school where Monroeville's residents considered themselves sophisticated compared to their rustic classmates. She particularly remembered a timid farm boy named Amos who would blush if a girl even spoke to him, perhaps becoming Harper Lee's model for Walter Cunningham. Louise took mischievous teenage pleasure in teasing Amos about his shyness. When Vanity Fair built a textile mill in Monroeville in 1937, becoming the county's largest employer, Amos took a job there. One day as Louise toured the new factory, she recognized him sitting at a machine sewing bras. Reverting to her teenage persona, she sidled up to him before he noticed and exclaimed, "Well, Amos!" They had not seen each other in two decades, but upon realizing that she had been watching his work on the intimates production line, he blushed as suddenly as he had as a youth.

Louise and Hershel Conner had two sons, Herschel H. III (Hank) and Edwin Lee (Ed). Hank followed his parents to Auburn University, completed a graduate degree from the University of Florida, then taught broadcast journalism there. Ed attended the University of the South at Sewanee, Tennessee, completed a PhD in literature at Vanderbilt, then taught the Great Books Program in the Honors College at Kentucky State University, a historically African American school. Both were voracious readers and protective of their Aunt Nelle's privacy. Following the deaths of Louise and Alice, Hank advised Nelle about publication of *Go Set a Watchman*.

YEARS OF SUNDAY VISITS with Louise in Eufaula, driving her to her favorite "meat and three" cafe across the state line in Lumpkin, Georgia, followed by afternoons on her back porch watching birds at the feeder when weather permitted, allowed us to swap family stories. During most of those years the one taboo subject was Harper Lee. We never asked about her, and Louise did not mention her except in passing. Mostly Louise talked about her father, describing him as an "inward Christian" who made no public display of his piety despite being a teetotaling Methodist and a resolutely upright man. She did not mention his blind spot regarding race, a common deficiency among Southern white Christians of his generation.

She described her mother as suffering from "nerve problems" which caused neighbors to complain when she woke them before dawn loudly playing classical music on her piano. Following multiple shock treatments in Mobile—the then-common regimen for what is now diagnosed as bipolar disorder—she spent many summers at Orange Beach on the Alabama Gulf Coast, where Louise and her three siblings would visit one at a time. Truman Capote later circulated absurd rumors, published by his biographer, that Mrs. Lee tried to drown Nelle in the bathtub. Actually, all three daughters adored their mother and denounced the gossip.

Hours of stories about the Finch, Flynt, Smith, and Lee

families seemed at first merely the genealogical accounts that flow like water from a spring in our part of the world. We longed for more than that. We have a saying in the South about strangers meeting. The Southerner asks, "Who are you?" The stranger says his name. The Southerner replies: "I didn't ask your name; I asked who you are." When we realized Louise wanted us to tell her who we were, in return for her similar revelation, we bought a journal and began recording stories.

Ellen Rivers Williams Finch, Louise's grandmother, was aristocratic and somewhat haughty despite declining family wealth from the plantation. Louise's mother, Frances Cunningham Finch Lee, was "spoiled by her raising" and education by private tutors at a school constructed in front of their house and attended by the two Finch sisters and a few white neighbor children.

Louise, nicknamed "Weezie," became a bit of a nonconformist among Eufaula's elite families, partly due to her upbringing in the Methodist church and somewhat due to the security provided by a successful businessman-husband. She sided with a racially moderate mayor, newspaper publisher, and educators who continued to support public schools following racial integration in the late 1960s.

When the city council subsequently appropriated two hundred thousand dollars to improve an African American neighborhood, the mayor asked Louise and her Methodist pastor to serve on a five-person biracial committee. They worked collaboratively with black activists organized under the title "Community on the Move," which had been formed by an African American woman to improve education and reduce drug abuse in the neighborhood. Louise remembered asking the woman at their first meeting:

"What can I do to help?" Her new friend hesitated, then initiated her into the complexities of racial transitions in Black Belt Alabama towns: "You have a white face!" She meant that only whites could lend legitimacy among other whites to blacks' demands for change. Members of the committee met weekly, ate together, and visited in each other's homes. Long after the civic initiative ended, Louise's African American friend continued to visit for coffee and conversation.

Louise also described a legendary visit in the 1960s by Nelle's first literary agent, Maurice Crain. He had expressed interest in seeing Nelle's world. Although a longtime resident of New York City, he was a Texan and maintained his Southern roots. He persuaded Nelle to fly with him to Atlanta where the family would meet them. Louise became nauseous from motion sickness (perhaps a symptom of Meniere's Disease, from which Dartie also suffered), but when she recovered, the sisters and Crain drove to Sewanee, Tennessee, to visit Ed, stopping en route at the Chickamauga Civil War battlefield where several of Crain's ancestors were buried. Although Crain was already ill with the cancer that would take his life several years later, the party especially enjoyed Clara's Castle, a hotel with a breathtaking view of a mountain cove. After a brief visit to Monroeville, they continued to Destin, Florida, for a three-day gulf vacation. When Crain returned to New York City, he told friends that "the three sisters agreed on nothing, argued about everything, laughed continuously, and everyone had a wonderful time." Having thoroughly sampled Louise's wit and wisdom by then, we did not doubt her story.

Of the three sisters, we concluded that Louise could deliver the cleverest one-line zingers. Once when we arrived at her house to drive her to a late lunch, she asked if we could wait until the closely contested British Open golf tournament was decided. Later as we were driving to lunch, she asked if we played golf. Neither of us did, nor did we know anything about the sport.

That was all the information she needed for a long disquisition about golf, the Lee family enthusiasm for it, and the traditions of the British Open. The tournament begins with a Scottish bagpiper playing the traditional Christian hymn, "Amazing Grace." Then she said what we considered at the time an afterthought but later concluded was an instruction: "When I die, I want a bagpiper to play 'Amazing Grace.' I won't know whether I'm in heaven or at the British Open, and it won't make any difference."

When we attended her funeral years later in Eufaula, the Lee family could find no bagpiper. But we were certain that her great-granddaughter's violin solo of the hymn was sufficiently haunting and beautiful.

Later in our friendship, as she greeted us in her hallway, I asked Louise about a color photograph of what appeared to be a two-story antebellum home. She identified it as her grandmother's ancestral home at Finchburg (although other family members later identi-fied it as the home of her Williams grandparents). Following a long pause, she then added: "Doty [Nelle's family nickname] doesn't want me to tell you about our family. She believes our friendship is just your way of finding out about her." We assured Louise that we found her fascinating and her sister aloof and preoccupied with her own life in New York City. Louise paused for a moment, grinned broadly, and said firmly: "Well, they were my parents too!" That is the day the family tales began to pour forth, with detailed charac-ter sketches and enthusiastic storytelling.

Months later Louise fell and broke a hip. She recuperated in assisted living, where we detected the early symptoms of dementia. Hank Conner insisted she move to Gainesville, Florida, to be close to him. She reacted like a typical Lee woman, telling Dartie: "I checked myself into this place and I can check myself out!" Despite Ed's invitation to live in Kentucky near him, she moved to Florida to be close to her older son and his family.

After her transfer to an assisted living facility in Gainesville, Hank asked us to call her, hoping she would recognize our voices. We tried, but tragically she had no memory of us. When we conveyed the news to Hank, he said sadly, "Then we have lost her."

ALICE LEE WAS FIFTEEN when Nelle was born and was approaching the century mark when we came to know her well. A tiny wisp of a woman, she seemed to survive on shrimp and oysters at David's Catfish Restaurant, in a state where fried catfish is sacrosanct. Even between ages 101 and 103, when she could barely whisper, she never wearied of telling us about Southwest Alabama. Her eyes would sparkle when she recognized our voices.

When we first met, Alice's voice was already shrill and raspy with a peculiar tremor. She could not hear even her own voice by then but had learned to lip-read. From her training in speech, Dartie could imitate her voice perfectly. I would try to describe it to friends only to be corrected by Dartie: "No, no, no, Wayne, that is not the way she sounds." Then she slowly and precisely repeated the words so expertly in tone, pace, and tremor that I would have sworn Alice had taken possession of Dartie's body. After a failed cochlear implant, Alice continued through her nineties spending her first hour in the office grasping the walls of a narrow back hallway and doing dance-like movements up and down the hall trying to improve her balance.

The constants in our afternoons with Alice until the last months of her life were her wit and memory. At age ninety-nine she arrived in Nelle's apartment with her driver late one afternoon after work. She greeted us by saying: "I knew you were here because I saw your '43' license plate." Each of Alabama's sixty-seven counties has a different license plate number prefix, but I knew Alice had never seen ours before nor had she lived even briefly anywhere except in Monroe, Montgomery, and Jefferson counties. Amazed as I often was at her mental acuity at such advanced age, I asked how she knew that "43" was the prefix for Lee County where we lived.

She explained slowly, precisely, and with a twinkle in her eyes that I will never forget: "I have insomnia. And when I can't sleep, I name the presidents of the United States in reverse order, then the vice presidents. Sometimes on really bad nights, I then repeat the counties and their tag numbers, beginning with Jefferson [as largest, number 1] and ending with Winston [67]. I never reach Winston because before then I fall asleep."

We looked at her with a mixture of awe and suspicion, but she only flashed a grin that ranged between angelic and demonic. We learned later that she could also repeat the names of all Alabama governors to date and their lieutenant governors.

Chapter 2

An Alabama Childhood/Education

WHEN THE STOCK MARKET CRASHED IN 1929, ALICE WAS EIGHTteen years old, Louise thirteen, and Nelle three. Until then they had experienced a childhood common to Southern whites in the times, though theirs was interrupted occasionally by their mother's bipolar disorder (even then she usually managed the household with the help of African American women who cooked and cleaned house).

The children's maternal grandparents in Finchburg and the place itself played a significant role in their childhoods. Nelle explained that although *Mockingbird* focused on her father's life, many of the family stories were derived from the Finches, who seemed to confirm local folklore that people born in Monroe County lived forever. Her grandmother Finch lived almost to ninety-four, her aunt to ninety-seven. Many of their distant neighbors, the Gaillards, lived beyond the century mark. Nelle explained one afternoon that there was a saying among men in the county: "Never marry a Gaillard woman because they live forever."

Alice spent miserable summer months in Finchburg because her grandmother would not allow her to play with black children despite their being the only available playmates. As the years passed, Mrs. Finch finally relented, even allowing Fanny, Alice's favorite African American playmate, into their house. Alice told us this story in a whisper lest Marcilla Harrington, her African American caregiver, overhear the conversation—which we were certain she already knew from the subterranean storytelling of black Monroe County women working for white Monroe County women, all of whom assumed interracial stories remained intra-racial.

The entire Lee family spent every Christmas at Finchburg, enthralled by steamboats on the Alabama River moving cargo to Mobile through the fog and mist of winter, the two-story Finch house aglow with Christmas lights and decorations. Louise memorialized her childhood by hanging the color photograph of the Finch home in her hallway in Eufaula. Nelle wrote two novels depicting Finchburg in the background of each.

As in most Southern childhoods, pets also played a role. Louise was a dog lover, Nelle preferred cats, and Alice was a neutral observer of animal life. Nelle insisted on assigning some metaphysical meaning to her preference, mainly for my benefit since I was a dog person. "We were cat people," she boasted. "Cats are independent! Cats are confident!" As for dogs, she added lest I had missed her point, they were "too dependent, don't take care of themselves, and are too much trouble." I had to bite my tongue to avoid the obvious reply: "It sounds to me as if you are distinguishing between women and men rather than cats and dogs."

She continued her disquisitions on cats by telling a story about her brother Ed's cat named "Teddy Rex" in honor of President Theodore Roosevelt. Ed had once thrown Teddy into the fireplace without distinguishing the cat from wooden toys which he routinely tossed into the fire to see them explode into flames. Singed but very much alive, Teddy emerged from the fireplace, ran to Ed, and slapped his face hard with a paw.

When Nelle was older, she began reading Ed's "Seckatary Hawkins" adventure books written by Robert F. Schulkers. She especially enjoyed *The Gray Ghost*, a mystery involving unfair accusations about an innocent man. *The Cadaver of Gideon Wyck*, a childhood book she reread throughout her life, combined science fiction, crime, and horror. As she matured, her focus shifted to Mark Twain's classics *Tom Sawyer* and *Huckleberry Finn*.

One afternoon she asked if we remembered a childhood book about a cannibal who ate a man. Since my childhood reading consisted exclusively of comic books and histories of the Civil War and Second World War, I joked that cannibalism was not my thing. Dartie ruined my strategy by admitting that she vaguely remembered such a book. Nelle apparently took notice of that afternoon and subsequently played clever mind games with us. They involved what appeared on the surface to be a genuine question but which always played to Dartie's reading interests rather than mine. I increasingly wondered if Nelle called Dartie and prearranged such scenarios.

UNFORTUNATELY, WHAT LITTLE OTHER writers have revealed about Nelle's childhood centers on her friendship with Truman Capote, the tree house her father built for them in the chinaberry tree in their yard, and his old typewriter which they hoisted up the tree and which inspired two brilliant careers. Their friendship was certainly her most important until it ended in acrimony during the

1960s. But Truman was only an episodic presence in her life, and Nelle's childhood proceeded fine without him.

Renowned Alabama storyteller Kathryn Tucker Windham, a frequent commentator on National Public Radio in the 1980s and 1990s, was a longtime friend of Nelle. One day we drove Kathryn to Monroeville so the two could visit. Our reward was an afternoon listening as two of Alabama's literary giants traded memories.

Kathryn was Nelle's senior by a few years, was as devout a Methodist as Alice, and was a graduate of Huntingdon College, the Methodist women's school in Montgomery. Kathryn told us she had learned from her college roommate that as a child Nelle had a mean streak. Kathryn's roommate—whose father had pastored Monroeville's Methodist church—had often babysat for Nelle. On one of those occasions, she had bitten the babysitter so hard that she bled, and the wound became infected. Decades later she claimed to be the only person in the world to have a signed copy of *Mockingbird* and a permanent scar inflicted by its author. We never saw Nelle have a better day than enjoying Kathryn's private performance.

Although Nelle loved and respected her father, brother Ed was her greatest hero. He took after their athletic father, served as captain of the high school football team, and was the Lees' best golfer. She and Alice ranked family golfing proficiency with Ed in first place, followed by Nelle, her father, Louise, and Alice. Nelle enjoyed playing all sports—the rougher, the better—but especially softball.

When not studying, reading, or playing sports in the late 1930s and early 1940s she escaped into the fantasies of the silver screen. Her favorite ten-cent movies during the Great Depression were Marx Brothers' comedies and later Humphrey Bogart films, especially *Casablanca* (1941) and *Key Largo* (1948) from which she quoted lines as long as we knew her.

Her love for literature owed most to Gladys Watson, who taught her tenth- and eleventh-grade English, and Ida Shomo, her twelfth-grade English teacher. Watson introduced her at sixteen or seventeen to Jane Austen's *Emma*, and she was hooked for life on the famous British novelist. The teachers also plunged her into Shakespeare's Elizabethan canon of plays. Like Nelle's, both of our high school English teachers had required memorization of long passages from Shakespeare.

Dartie and Nelle remembered the lines, but I had long since buried the Bard under mountains of Alabama history. This fact furnished Harper her favorite malicious mischief. When conversation about some particularly mendacious American politician or celebrity scandal lagged, she reverted to what in the beginning seemed a genuine plea for help with failing memory. She would quote a passage from Shakespeare, pretend forgetfulness, look squarely at me, and ask: "What play contained that passage, Wayne?" At first, I responded that I had no idea, but she was relentless. Rather than face monthly humiliation, I began to guess randomly *Hamlet, Macbeth, King Lear, A Midsummer Night's Dream*. According to her, I never guessed the correct play. Even worse, she would then turn to Dartie and ask if Dartie remembered. Whatever play Dartie named, Nelle pronounced as the correct answer. Never a single miss in years of contests. What are the odds? It took a long time for me to realize they were playing with my mind. Or, perhaps she genuinely could not remember and just picked on me. Or, as I became more paranoid, did the two conspire by phone while I was teaching my classes at Auburn, and the whole affair was their revenge on men?

I finally diverted the conversations by asking: "How can you remember all those passages?" She replied: "It's because Gladys Watson taught me to love Shakespeare. She was the best teacher I ever had. She read *Macbeth* aloud to us."

Uncommon among Southern teenagers growing up in a prim and proper county-seat town, Nelle called her parents, their adult friends, and even teachers by their given names. Among precocious children in private settings, the habit seemed innocent enough, perhaps even cute. But in public it made a child seem impudent or at least impolite. Nelle only slipped once, but it was a colossal mistake. She began a question to Mrs. Watson with "Gladys." Her teacher's icy stare triggered an immediate reaction: "Pardon, Mrs. Watson."

Two years of Watson's discipline and enthusiasm prepared her for Shomo, who came from a Monroe County community named for her ancestors. It is easy to ignore the pivotal nurturing of such teachers in the maturation of a person. Nelle never did. She visited Watson and Shomo whenever she was in Monroeville and remained friends with them while they still lived. Following the commercial success of *Mockingbird*, Nelle paid most of Watson's expenses on a trip to England to explore firsthand the literary world she conveyed to students. To maximize her time in London, Watson flew there. Because of her motion sickness, Nelle always traveled on the *Queen Mary* or the *Queen Elizabeth*. She ended her rhapsodic account of that sea crossing with one of her signature postscripts about the nauseous boredom of air travel compared to passage aboard elegant cruise ships: "Orville and Wilbur Wright be damned!" Watson and Lee rendezvoused in London and set out for Shakespeare country. Years later, when Nelle told us about the experience, her voice trembled a bit after a long pause: "Gladys talked about that trip for the rest of her life."

Nelle had another, if less likely, favorite, Eloise Bell, who taught eleventh-grade physics. When the movie *To Kill a Mockingbird* premiered at Mobile's finest theater, Nelle rented a limousine to transport her former teacher to and from the movie. According to Bell's son, it was one of the highlights of her life.

LIKE MOST SOUTHERN FAMILIES, Nelle's parents relied on genealogy and family stories to convey what they thought children needed to know about ancestors. Her father's most memorable stories concerned his father, Cader Alexander Lee, who died on October 9, 1910, only months before Alice's birth.

Nelle did not relish genealogy as much as her father and Alice did, nor were any of the family obsessed with the Civil War. I attributed that to their extraordinarily long lives. Firsthand memories of wars, especially such as that one, require lots of recovery time before they can be shared. The longevity of the family meant that Alice heard stories about her grandfather not many years after he died, and Louise, Ed, and Nelle heard them within the next couple of decades. Nelle's accounts of the decisive second day of the Battle of Gettysburg chilled my blood a century and a half later, so I can imagine how searing it must have been close to Cader Lee's death.

Nelle told us a slimmed-down version of the story on February 2, 2015. Both the date and context are significant. National media were dominated by news about the "discovery" of the manuscript of her first novel, *Go Set a Watchman*. Disputes about the discovery of the manuscript, its provenance, and Nelle's mental capacity to approve its publication raged for months thereafter. Various persons for their own reasons promoted fantastical conspiracy theories: Nelle was locked away in assisted living; she was suffering from dementia and incapable of giving informed consent about anything; she was being manipulated by her avaricious attorney. Central to all these conspiracies was Nelle's mental capacity. Other than Dartie and I, her nephews and a niece, her physician, attorney Tonja Carter, and a few close female friends she dubbed "The Usual Suspects," almost no one even saw or talked with Nelle, much less could offer informed diagnosis of her cognitive ability.

The afternoon began with my childhood story about my sharecropper grandfather. Following a lifetime of plowing, planting, cultivating, fertilizing, and picking cotton, he quit the land and moved into his own house, built by my father and his seven siblings on the "Buttermilk Road" near my hometown of Anniston.

Nelle interrupted the story to make sure she had heard correctly the "Buttermilk Road." "Correct," I answered. It received its unofficial name from dairies, one owned by my relatives. In family lore, my grandfather joked that the road was so deeply rutted and poorly maintained that when a dairyman started to Anniston with containers of milk, the cream separated and by the time he arrived in town the milk had been churned into buttermilk. It took her a while to process the humor, so I changed the subject and asked if her grandfather drank buttermilk. "I reckon so," she laughed, "because he was raised on a farm." That was my last interruption of the story she told about Cader Lee.

NEAR THE BEGINNING OF the Civil War, Cader and his brother Timothy enlisted as privates in Company H of the 15th Alabama Infantry Regiment, whose second and final commander was Colonel William Oates. Rather than glorifying the event involving her grandfather, she told us that he and his brother "ran fast and were neither killed nor wounded." She followed that cryptic sentence with an eruption of laughter. Given her satirical account of his conduct, I thought it inappropriate to pose the question of what she meant by it until I had done some homework. I knew the name William Oates because he was elected governor of Alabama in 1894, within the span of my historical expertise. But I knew nothing about his military career.

Cader, Timothy, and most of their comrades lived in southeastern Alabama in Barbour County, where Louise Lee Conner settled, or Dale County where Cader and Timothy Lee lived. The two counties, though spatially close, were worlds apart economically. Barbour anchored the eastern end of Alabama's Black Belt and produced much of its cotton. Nearly half the county's white population owned slaves, so they had a significant economic stake in the outcome of the war.

The soil in Dale County in the Wiregrass region to the south was not well-suited to cotton. Farmers there mostly practiced subsistence agriculture on small farms and raised cattle and swine on the open range. In 1860, less than 20 percent of Dale's white families owned even a single slave. Nearly half of all whites were poor. They were, per a popular local self-description, "the hardy sons of toil" rather than plantation aristocrats. Nonetheless, many of these poor people enlisted in the Confederate Army, perhaps because they hoped to become slave owners, or from some combination of pride, honor, and adventure.

Before the war ended four years later, their regimental flag listed many of the bloodiest battles in the eastern theater of the war: Cold Harbor; Malvern Hill; Manassas; Sharpsburg (Antietam); Fredericksburg; Gettysburg; Chickamauga. The regiment earned its nickname "Oates Tigers." Late in the war, Oates lost an arm to a Federal shell, and following the war he wrote a memoir describing July 2, 1863, at Gettysburg, Pennsylvania.

On that blistering hot day, the 520 Alabamians under Oates's command marched double-time twenty miles carrying rifles and heavy packs to reach the unfolding battle at midday. They were given no time to refill canteens before being ordered into combat. Above them, the Union Army's 20th Maine Regiment, commanded by seminarian and college professor Colonel Joshua Chamberlain, occupied two rocky crags named Big and Little Round Top, the most elevated terrain of the Gettysburg battlefield. When the Alabamians finally fought their way through a thick forest, a maze of boulders, and murderous gunfire, both regiments were exhausted and out of ammunition. They continued the battle hand-to-hand, using bayonets, knives, even rifles as clubs. Civil War historians describe the extended fighting at Gettysburg as the "High Water Mark of the Confederacy," ending when the exhausted remnant of the 15th Alabama broke and ran for their lives around boulders down the mountain. Documentary filmmaker Ken Burns lionized Colonel Chamberlain, who was killed in the action for which he was awarded the Congressional Medal of Honor.

William Oates's younger brother was also killed. Cader Lee's uncle was captured and died in a prisoner-of-war camp. Half their Confederate comrades were killed, wounded, or captured. During four years of fighting, the 15th Alabama suffered more casualties than any other regiment in Brigadier General McIver Law's famous Alabama Brigade, and Oates boasted after the war that his Alabamians fought more fiercely than Robert E. Lee's Virginians. That may have been true, at least on that memorable day. As Law's Alabama Brigade advanced, it wheeled to the left hitting the western slope of Little Round Top and threatening the Union left flank. General James Longstreet described the advance as the best three hours of fighting ever conducted by any troops on any battlefield.

That was the heroic ancestral story Nelle could have told, one which historians and documentary film makers have enshrined in history. She simplified the Confederates' fate: "They ran fast and were neither killed nor wounded." The next time we visited her, armed with the rest of the story, I asked how Cader had survived without a wound when half his comrades were killed, wounded, or captured. She would not take my bait. "I guess he could run faster." As we traveled home late that afternoon, I told Dartie that I had never known a Southerner with such a heroic ancestral story who so completely demythologized the Confederate military. Rather than venerate Confederate ancestors, Nelle gently satirized them for breaking and running instead of fighting and dying. But it was also clear that she respected honorable ancestors on the wrong side of history.

AFTER THE WAR, CADER Lee married Theodocia Euphrasia Windham—a name that never failed to bring smiles to the three sisters when they pronounced or spelled it—and later moved to Butler County in the center of the Black Belt, where Nelle's father was born, the youngest of nine children. Cader Lee next moved the family to the Florida panhandle (nicknamed "Lower Alabama" by their neighbors to the north), faithfully attended the Methodist church, was elected to the Florida state legislature, and served a term as mayor of Graceville.

Their son, Amasa Coleman ("Coley") Lee was talented in math and went far enough in school to become an accountant for the Bear Creek Lumber Company near Finchburg, Alabama. Louise described him as tall and athletic, especially in baseball. Most small towns in that era fielded teams, and Coley pitched for Finchburg. In a game against the Bear Creek team, he pitched against his boss who owned the company. He pondered whether to serve up a powder-puff pitch or try to strike out his boss. He struck him out. Louise considered that an omen of things to come in terms of his personal honor. He also met and married Frances Cunningham Finch and settled in Monroeville.

Coley was, Louise told us, a "sociable, outgoing" man who was always interested in politics, like his father before him. If inclined to such a career, the first step in Alabama was a law degree. With a new wife and no money, leaving for law school was not an option, so he "read" law, learning enough from books to pass the state bar exam. As teacher, accountant, and attorney, he dressed the roles. His grandson, Hank Conner, remembered Coley Lee always wearing a suit, vest, and tie, with his pocket watch hanging on a chain from his vest pocket. In time he prospered sufficiently to buy the local newspaper, which he also edited. He was elected to the Alabama legislature and was mentioned among possible aspirants for the governorship. If the father was bigger than life, the mother often disappeared into the shadows of her disease.

After receiving her diploma from Monroe County High School, Nelle followed in the path of her oldest sister, Alice, to Methodist Huntingdon College in Montgomery. That decision did not turn out well. In the 1940s Southern world of blousy skirts, bobby socks, lots of makeup, and casual flirtations between coeds and older men in or just out of military service, Nelle wore Bermuda shorts, cursed, smoked, and preferred golf to dating. Whether Nelle was encouraged by pious Methodist officials to transfer, as rumors allege, or just hated to be told how to dress, talk, and act, as she claimed, is a matter of dispute. That she joyfully transferred to the University of Alabama is not.

Life at the "Capstone," as the university in Tuscaloosa was known, began no better than at Huntingdon. She made a strategic mistake by joining the Chi Omega sorority when education in the 1940s was as much about making strategic connections to influential Alabama families as it was about obtaining knowledge and degrees. Furthermore, walking through the intensely social lounge of the Chi Omegas in her Bermuda shorts and carrying her golf clubs on Saturday mornings made her as much an embarrassment to sorority sisters as she had been to Methodist students at Huntingdon.

Soon enough she discovered friends in the offices of *The Crimson-White* campus paper and the *Rammer Jammer* humor/literary magazine. High school English teachers and her preference for writing inclined her toward the Shakespeare class taught by legendary professor Hudson Strode, a well-regarded biographer of Jefferson Davis among other books. But he was something of a showman whom she considered egotistical, self-absorbed, and a fraud. His class did inspire one of Nelle's finest parodies about the writing life. Her story "The Writer" was published in the November 1945 issue of the *Rammer Jammer*. She satirized one of Strode's acolytes who was fond of framing writers inside stereotypical categories:

"How do you like sex?" he inquired one day as they walked out of class.

"I said I liked it very well."

"I don't," he replied. "Sex has been run in the ground."

Without a segue, he moved on to his next question, asking if she were an atheist.

"No," she replied, disappointing him again.

"I had thought you showed some spark of intelligence," he told her dismissively, "but I see that you are just another one of the cattle. Good day, Miss Lee."

The rest of the essay was a satire on the requisites of The Writer: a sadistic father; an abusive, alcoholic mother; mistreatment by older siblings; all of these fortunately bequeathing The Writer an unhappy childhood. "Soul" was imperative as well, but not just any soul. Frustrated, "somnambulistic" or warped souls worked best. Sexual frustrations were particularly desirable. Self-love, cursing God "at regular intervals," and scorn from people one loved the most added valuable elements to The Writer's assets. The Writer's environment was equally important. The most useful background was a small town, preferably a Southern village. Annual violent race riots helped, as did Pentecostal or Holiness tent meetings on the edge of town. Crooked judges, dilapidated court houses, and "immoral goings-on" added color and generated momentum for reform movements committed to doing away with small towns altogether. Finally, The Writer's Bohemian lifestyle—even if artificially enhanced by "Benzedrine parties, sinful living, and alcoholic benders"—although not necessarily his preferred vices—were necessary elements of his research. "He thereby sacrifices his virtue in order to give the American public 'The Truth'." Following his premature death, his "cast-off mistresses" would divide his royalties.

If Georgia novelist Erskine Caldwell—who specialized in fiction about such places and people—had read Nelle's essay, he would have recognized himself in nearly every paragraph. Fortunately, Professor Strode presumably did not read her parody, or if he did, dismissed it as typical sophomoric and ribald undergraduate *Rammer Jammer* humor not necessarily directed at him.

Although she declared her major as the university's five-year law school curriculum, she elaborated on that choice in a 1963 news conference in Chicago promoting the film adaptation of *Mockingbird*. A reporter asked her about the Lee family's legal tradition and her law school studies at the university. As in most interviews during the brief span when she allowed them, she did not equivocate in her answer: "For three years I had to study something in college, and I grew up in a legal household. The minute, though, that I started to study law, I loathed it. I always wanted to be a writer."

She did form life-long friendships with other students interested in writing and enjoyed participating in intramural athletics and attending Alabama football games. But given that she did not enjoy sorority life or Hudson Strode, dropped out of the five-year law school curriculum without a degree, and moved to New York City, I always marveled at her fierce allegiance to the University of Alabama. Furthermore, her brother Ed and sister Louise graduated from Auburn. Nelle was the outlier in the family, as I often reminded her. None of that made any difference in our friendship, though it did enliven our afternoons during football season.

ON DECEMBER 6, 2013, I persuaded Dartie that we HAD to visit Nelle before Christmas so I could deliver my Auburn holiday gift. On Thanksgiving weekend, Auburn's football team had upset the heavily favored Crimson Tide in what Alabamians call the annual "Iron Bowl." Auburn had not just beaten Alabama but had beaten them in a way unprecedented in football history. I had been sitting in my priority seat on the twenty-yard line—after nearly forty years of purchasing season tickets and mostly watching us lose to our cross-state rival.

First, I would carefully reconstruct the events. Score tied. One second left. Legendary coach Nick Saban called a time out to consider his final play. He could put his kicker in the game to try a long field goal. If successful, they win. Or, he could let the time expire and go to overtime. He decided to try the kick. It had plenty of distance but sailed slightly right of the goal. An Auburn player caught the ball and returned it 109 yards for the upset win. Auburn students and even old men and women who knew better began to plunge through a boundary of hedges and onto the field where they dodged goal posts being torn down.

I wore my Auburn University sweater and carefully rehearsed the final seconds of the game all the way to Monroeville while Dartie scolded me for driving too fast. I tried to explain as rationally as possible that I was about to erase decades of humiliation, which Dartie, who neither knew nor cared about football, could not possibly understand.

Within two minutes of our arrival, Nelle had demolished my carefully constructed assault with her own obviously well-rehearsed preemptive strike. In the lobby filled with residents, visitors and staff, she was waiting for us in her wheelchair, dressed in a Crimson Tide sweater and white pedal pushers, flashing a Cheshire cat grin. Before I could say a word, she began a chant: "Alabama, Alabama, by the Black Warrior River, Love you with my heart and love you with my liver." After a moment of stunned silence processing what she had just said—while Dartie collapsed in laughter onto the couch beside her—I sputtered that the stupid chant sounded like a typical sophomoric cheer from the 1940s. Furthermore, she should be dressed in sack cloth and ashes as the Bible commanded for people in mourning. Unruffled, she subjected me to an encore performance.

Dartie tried to change the subject. Thinking about Nelle's chronic hearing problems, she asked loudly, "How are you doing?" Looking straight at Dartie and away from me, she shouted so all could hear: "I wasn't feeling well, but I feel wonderful now that YOU are here."

Three months later, and assuming that media accounts of her memory loss were accurate, we returned. As I walked into her apartment, she ambushed me with "Alabama, Alabama, . . ." and the same wicked grin.

Of all the famous people Nelle met in her remarkable life, only three filled her with awe: Groucho Marx, President Lyndon Johnson, and Alabama football coach Paul "Bear" Bryant. The legendary coach arrived in Tuscaloosa a decade after she left for New York. Following many victories and national football championships, administrators and alumni hosted a banquet in his honor at the Plaza Hotel in New York City and invited Nelle, who had won the Pulitzer Prize but did not know the Bryants well. Unlike her undergraduate days at the university, she was dressed elegantly in honor of him and the event. Extremely nervous, as she always was on such occasions, she waited impatiently for the elevator. When the door finally opened, she stood face to face with Coach Bryant and Mary Harmon, his wife. Before she could regain her composure, Bryant looked at his wife and muttered in his famous, raspy, deep voice, "Well, Mother, Harper Lee is here. Now we can begin."

Chapter 3

Three Anglophiles

WE NEVER BOTHERED TO ASK NELLE OR HER SISTERS HOW THEY obtained their nicknames. Louise volunteered that Alice was called "Bear" because her parents took her to the Montgomery zoo during a legislative session, and she admired an ancient bear. Louise was called "Weezie" as a phonetic rendering of her real name. But the origin of Nelle's nickname, "Doty," is more obscure. The family members we asked about it were uncertain, but her nephew Ed Conner speculated that it may have been a product of the family's proud English origins.

A version of Doty (alternatively spelled "Doughty" and "Dohti") appeared in Bedfordshire in 1247 and was common in Yorkshire in the fourteenth century. The ancient Anglo-Saxon word meant brave, strong, valiant, hardy, and manly, all of which described Nelle. We also considered the possibility that the cerebral Truman Capote may have selected the nickname, or, given her affection for all things British, she may have chosen it herself. When I heard her lecture in Eufaula where she proclaimed Lord McCaulay her favorite historian, I was even more convinced of her Anglophile tendencies. Although I did not share her affection for him, I was a fan of C. S. Lewis. And William Shakespeare was her favorite lay theologian and dramatist.

Nelle's reluctance to fly because of motion sickness afforded us an advantage in our mutual Anglophilia because we frequently flew to the United Kingdom. She relished accounts of our travels, and we always shared our stories and souvenirs. After her stroke, these provided vicarious journeys to some of her favorite places.

An uptick in American studies programs in the U.K. during the late twentieth century, increasing faculty exchanges between U.S. and British professors, reduced airline prices due to more competition, and creation of the European Southern Studies Association, brought invitations for me to lecture in every part of the U.K. and western Europe: at Queens University in Belfast, Northern Ireland; at the universities of Newcastle, Sussex, Oxford, and Cambridge, in the U.K.; at the University of Vienna and in Prague; at the Franklin Roosevelt Center in the Netherlands.

After my retirement in 2005, we extended lectureships into month-long adventures or even three-month visiting professorships. I became experienced at renting cars and driving on the "wrong" side of England's back roads. Many of those wanderings were revelatory. While visiting friends, we hiked through what remains of Old Sarum, the earliest site of modern Salisbury and its magnificent cathedral. As early as 400 BC, when ancient druids first appeared in Roman accounts as religious leaders and recorders of lore, wandering tribes erected an Iron Age hill fort where two paths intersected near the monoliths of Stonehenge and Avebury, both places of mystery and vague unease after dark.

The day we traipsed across Old Sarum, we imagined the thrill Gladys Watson must have experienced as Nelle explained how she had repurposed and relocated the ancient druid world of proud, clannish people into the "enormous and confusing tribe" that settled "Old Sarum" in her fictional Maycomb County, Alabama. I had already concluded that the Red Hills would have been the perfect location for subsistence farmers who preserved ancient ways of settling grudges, clan solidarity, and even a barter system during the Great Depression. The ethnic pride, honor, and independence of such people manifested itself in the trial of Tom Robinson when the last holdout juror against the death penalty was a Cunningham from "Old Sarum." Ed Conner speculated that naming a poor white family for her pretentious grandmother was a sly dig at Nelle's snobbish Williams family and a nod to people like those of Old Sarum.

During the summer of 1947 Nelle attended a student exchange program at Oxford University. Her course in Twentieth Century Europe and opportunities to travel by train and on foot confirmed her love for England and her discomfort at any more time wasted in Alabama's law school.

Nelle's times in England contained surprises beyond just place names for her novels. During her return voyage on the *Queen Mary* following one of her trips with Gladys Watson, she met an elderly man at her dinner table. He introduced himself as "Mr. Wilberforce." She astounded him by asking if he might be related to the eighteenth-century abolitionist William Wilberforce. "He was my grandfather!" the surprised man replied. On our drive home the day Nelle told us about that, Dartie and I speculated about the ensuing table conversation and whether he had read *Mockingbird*. If so, had he recognized the reference to Old Sarum? Did they discuss race relations or other English abolitionists such as the Methodist Wesley brothers?

In June 2012, Dartie and I reprised one of Nelle's trips. Traveling on the *Queen Mary II* during its crossing in celebration of Queen Elizabeth's Diamond Jubilee, we made landfall in Southhampton just ahead of the *Queen Victoria* and *Queen Elizabeth II.* A thousand smaller vessels crowded the harbor and the Queen herself greeted us from a platform set up for the occasion. We joined thousands of passengers on the top deck shouting "God save the Queen," "Hip, hip, hurrah," and singing "Rule Britannia."

Following the festivities, we drove our rental car to nearby Winchester Cathedral where Jane Austen is buried. After paying homage, we continued on to the tiny village of Chawton where her father was Anglican vicar and where she grew up. We spent most of a day in the vicarage, which now serves as an excellent Jane Austen museum and interpretive center. Wherever we traveled on our Jane Austen pilgrimage, even to London's British Museum which displays her writing desk and some of her handwritten manuscripts, we were aware that Nelle had preceded us.

WE RETURNED TO MONROEVILLE and The Meadows with Sainsbury Tea purchased in Winchester and two Union Jacks waved in honor of the Queen, and then we three Anglophiles sang an impromptu rendition of "Rule Britannia" so loudly that Nelle's fellow assisted-living residents must have wondered whether we were drunk, had lost our minds, or a British invasion of Monroe County was underway.

We also brought her a birthday gift, a copy of *The Real Jane Austen,* a superb new biography of her favorite author published during the run-up to Austen's two hundredth birthday celebration. It was our most appreciated present ever. We had read it first and agreed that Byrnes's portrayal of Austen offered clues to Nelle's life, philosophy, and fiction writing.

Born in 1775, one of eight children, Austen turned down a marriage proposal as a young woman, preferring the financially precarious option of remaining a single female writer caring for herself. When she died at age forty-one, the obituary written by her brother mentioned her charity, religious devotion, and personal purity, but not her six novels whose global popularity earned her sufficient fame that her likeness is on the British ten-pound note. Each epoch since Austen's death has resulted in a new international audience which discovers different meaning in her life that parallels generational changes in how she is perceived.

Austen's new style of realism, which moved deftly between a narrator's voice and a character's innermost feelings, mesmerized readers. Lee used it effectively in *Mockingbird*. Such indirect speech allows the reader to see, think, and feel what the fictional character experiences while maintaining the capacity to move back and forth between the viewpoints of narrator and actor.

In the twentieth century, the women's suffrage movement and the "new woman" laid claim to Austen. Readers reimagined her as a "demure rebel" subverting the established social order from within female respectability.

During two world wars, audiences were drawn to the comfort, stability, and eternal values embedded in Austen's stories. Her warm family narratives offered sanctuary and reassurance to a world gone mad. In the 1990s, British and American film producers stripped the narrator out of Austen's novels and substituted more female sexuality.

Through two centuries of shifting and conflicted interpretations about the meaning of Austen's life and fiction, her fame did not wane, as Byrnes's biography made clear in references to the Jane Austen Society of Japan, her books' popularity in China and India, not to mention the popular American movie *The Jane Austen Book Club.* As a writer for *The Economist* wrote in the year of her bicentenary: "Austen's sniping observations of human vanity and folly still hit the mark."

Austen parallels to Lee's life and fiction are too numerous to have been accidental. Harper used the literary voice of a narrator to great effect in *Mockingbird,* although that format was deleted from some stage adaptations. Generational perceptions of the meaning of *Mockingbird* changed just as they had for Austen's works. *Mockingbird* initially was received as the story of a courageous Southern lawyer defending the innocence of a black man when no other white attorney would take the case. Changing racial perceptions in America transformed Atticus Finch into a quasi-racist, ironically exacerbated by the discovery of Lee's own denunciation of her father-figure in the 1957 manuscript that was published finally as *Go Set a Watchman.*

When we presented *The Real Jane Austen* to Nelle, I suggested that Austen was the forerunner of her own fiction. I defended my presumptuousness by noting the obvious: her use of a narrator; her depiction of strong female characters such as Jean Louise ("Scout"), Miss Maudie Atkinson, and Calpurnia; female sexuality (Mayella Ewell's lust for a black man and false accusation of rape); and contrived female "sensibility" (Aunt Alexandra).

Nelle demurred until I read her back to her what she had written just after publication of *Mockingbird* describing her vision for the novel:

I would like to leave some record of the kind of life that existed in a very small world. I hope . . . to chronicle something that seems to be very quickly going down the drain. This is small-town middle-class Southern life as opposed to Gothic, as opposed to *Tobacco Road*, as opposed to plantation life.

There is a very definite social pattern in these towns that fascinates me. I think it is a rich social pattern. I would simply like to put down all I know about this because I believe that there is something universal in this little world, something decent to be said for it, and something to lament in its passing.

In other words, all I want to be is the Jane Austen of south Alabama.

She never explained beyond what she wrote then and what she said about small towns within her 1945 essay, "The Writer," in the *Rammer Jammer*. I suppose that said all that needed saying.

Chapter 4

Honest to God

ALTHOUGH ALICE AND LOUISE WERE RENOWNED IN THEIR RESPEC-
tive towns for piety and civic virtue, Nelle managed to avoid both.
After a lifetime responding to middle school teachers who sent her
boxes of student letters typically describing their favorite characters in *Mockingbird,* while living in Monroeville's assisted living
facility she refused to read any more. When the director of the
local museum dispatched me with the last large box of letters sent
to Harper Lee in care of the museum, Nelle told me what she
increasingly told everyone asking for an autograph, letter, or interview: "Hell, no!"

Despite her understandable displeasure at being subjected to
such burdens in her eighties, while partially paralyzed and increasingly blind and deaf, she possessed a kinder and softer persona
that few witnessed. During an Alabama Humanities Foundation award ceremony honoring Nelle, our mutual friend Nancy
Anderson observed her closely at the fund-raising reception. A
woman and her young daughter seemed out of place, their plain
dresses suggesting the mother might have spent more than she
could afford for tickets to the event. They seemed to know no
one there. The daughter carried a copy of *Mockingbird* despite
prominent signs—perhaps demanded by Nelle—warning: "No

photographs! No autographs!" When Nelle spotted the ador-
ing mother and excited daughter wandering across the crowded
room, she made her way to them and asked the girl if she wanted
her book signed. Noticing the mother's camera, she told her she
could take a photograph.

We witnessed many such incidents of kindness during our
years of friendship. The gruff exterior obscured the essence of the
woman. Wesleyan piety and personal kindness could survive even
long residence in New York City.

Often in close friendships, topics left unmentioned are as
important as those discussed, especially if faith is involved. Full
of stereotypes about religion in general and Baptists in particular, Nelle often chided me: "Wayne, you're too intelligent to be a
Baptist!" She spoke the words partly in jest but they still stung.
Baptists are like Pentecostals, Jews, Muslims, atheists, and even
Methodists. They come in all shapes and sizes, from varying back-
grounds, and with different educations, sensibilities, temperaments, and beliefs.

Nonetheless, religion as context and background was seldom
absent from our afternoons together. On one of our early visits
at Lakeshore Rehabilitation—when her prognosis, independence,
and future residence were all uncertain—we brought her our CD
player and a CD of the brilliant English comic/satirist John Cleese
reading *The Screwtape Letters*, C. S. Lewis's hilarious masterpiece
about Satan's pitch to a prospective convert. We learned that she
was a tremendous fan of Cleese and Lewis.

We also knew from *Mockingbird* her characterization of Jean
Louise Finch's Aunt Alexandra as a hypocrite who raised money
for Methodist missionaries in China, but refused to welcome their

converts to Maycomb's Methodist church. She also denounced Scout's first-grade teacher for misunderstanding her friend, Walter Cunningham, because he came from a poor white family in "Old Sarum."

Perhaps portrayals of Atticus Finch in two novels and of Coley Lee in family lore should be a constant reminder that most people think of religious faith as a process, not an event. When Louise Conner described her father as an "inward Christian," she meant that he was not inclined to ask people whether they were "saved," but that he took seriously the question, "What would Jesus do?" No one answers that question perfectly, and on race Coley Lee strayed wide of the right answer. In that regard he let his culture speak louder than his conscience. But considering the times in which he lived, his vision of racial justice was the norm regardless of the region of America under the historical microscope. Blacks living in Harlem during the 1930s did not regard New York City as the "New Jerusalem."

Then, of course, in *Go Set a Watchman* Nelle excoriates her father-figure for moving too slowly toward justice. The title itself offers insight to her religious upbringing and sensibilities. She chose it from Isaiah 21: 2–7, one of the most obscure passages in the Bible. I never knew a preacher who selected it for a text. Before publication of her novel, it was virtually never quoted in sermon anthologies.

That caused me to think about how she chose it. She could have been struck with the prophetic words and thought they could be spun into a story more relevant to her own time. It is less likely that she wrote the novel, then searched for a biblical text. It is least likely that she got out her King James Version (KJV) of the

Bible, closed her eyes, opened the Bible, placed her finger on the page, opened her eyes, and shouted, "Eureka! I've found it!" The most likely option is that she remembered the text well enough from reading it to know it provided a biblical introduction for what she wanted to write.

The KJV was the only translation she possessed because she believed it contained the classical language of highest English culture. I told her that in my class on the Hebrew Bible, Isaiah 2 was called a "Jeremiad," named for the ancient prophet's denunciation of social injustice and personal wickedness. In the 1950s and 1960s many Christians began describing Southern apartheid and racial injustice that way, so a biblical title seemed entirely appropriate for her novel.

To confirm that this episode was not a one-off example of biblical interpretation, I asked which book of the Bible was her favorite. Without hesitation she answered, "Exodus." "Why Exodus?" I asked. "Because they're leaving," she said firmly without further explanation.

Driving home that day, the more we considered her three-word answer, the more complicated it became. Was she thinking of the Hebrew exodus from Egyptian captivity? Or her own flight from Monroeville and Alabama? She had raised the question in *Watchman* when twenty-six-year-old Jean Louise Finch weighs her love for her fiancé and father against spending the rest of her life in Maycomb, Alabama:

"When you live in New York you often have the feeling that New York's not the world. . . every time I come home, I feel like I'm coming back to the world. It's silly. I can't explain it, and what makes it sillier is that I'd go stark raving mad living in Maycomb."

Her Maycomb-rooted fiancé, Henry Clinton, made her choice clear: "Sooner or later you will have to decide whether it's Maycomb or New York." Her decision will seal a fictional marriage or end a romance. And perhaps it settled more than that for her, as in where she would spend the rest of her life.

We concluded that Exodus was her favorite book of the Bible because at a critical juncture in her life, it had pointed the way to her most important decision, which is not an unusual reason for loving a book one considers to be sacred.

So FAR AS WE knew, she was never institutionally religious after leaving for college except when visiting home, when she sat in the family pew on the left side of the church. Before her stroke, she flaunted her smoking, drinking, ribald sense of humor, and, in *Watchman*, her astounding mastery of profanity.

She also knew how to demolish sanctimonious people. She delighted in telling a story about the president of Huntingdon College. Already unhinged from small-town Methodist piety, she did not conform to the social restrictions of a Methodist women's college either. Decades later, a friend wrote her that the new college president had claimed while speaking to an alumnae meeting that Harper Lee had left Huntingdon because she was expelled for smoking. Nelle wrote the president that she was not expelled for smoking, that the president at the time also smoked, and he should "cease and desist spreading lies" about her because it "was not Christian." Several weeks later, she received a contrite letter of apology.

Still later, when she rightfully could have claimed a significant act of piety, she satirized the event. At Alice's urging, she contributed a significant amount of money to construct a spacious fellowship hall adjacent to Monroeville Methodist Church. When she returned for the dedication of the building, she sat next to the pastor before the service began. When she excused herself to go to the bathroom, the pastor called to her: "Miss Lee, you forgot your purse." As she disappeared out the door, she replied: "I don't need it. Alice gave away all my money for this building!"

Despite her departure from conventional religion, Nelle's personal faith was a more complex matter. For one thing, there was her belief in racial justice, evident not only in novels but in her ridicule of Governor George C. Wallace and affection for Lady Bird and Lyndon Johnson. Johnson's 1964 Public Accommodations Act, 1965 Voting Rights Act, and early childhood education legislation was the most sweeping social justice reform since Abraham Lincoln's Emancipation Proclamation. She determined such political preferences by her internal moral compass.

Georgia native Flannery O'Connor—devout Catholic and brilliant author of Southern Gothic short stories and novels—explained her own fiction this way: "To those who are hard of hearing, we shout, and for those almost blind, we draw large and startling figures." She could have been describing *Mockingbird* and *Watchman*. Robert E. Lee Ewell, Atticus Finch, Calpurnia, Tom Robinson—all fit that time in America. Harper Lee "shouted." She drew "large and startling figures." In *Watchman* she also allowed her Uncle Jack to speak for her about the elemental way America must move toward racial justice: "Every man's island, Jean Louise, is his conscience." Not law. Not institutional religion. Not family. Not friends, or neighbors or townspeople. Only one's internal sense of fairness, equity, and justice. Legislation can change conduct. It does not ensure justice.

Not until the afternoon when we visited her on my birthday in 2014 did we discover the antecedents of her moral compass and their confluence with ours. Of course, there were her family and early Methodism. But a graduate seminar in moral theology rested heavily on the ottoman in her apartment. When I lifted the huge book, I discovered that it was an anthology of the writings of C. S. Lewis. I stupidly asked if she were a Lewis fan. "Of course!" she answered, then elaborated: "The greatest Christian apologist since St. Augustine's *Confessions*."

"What are your favorite C. S. Lewis books?" I continued. "*Mere Christianity* and *Surprised by Joy*," she replied. Because these were also my favorite Lewis books, we knew the agenda for the afternoon.

Ironically, Dartie and I had recently returned from England, where I had lectured at Sidney Sussex College, Cambridge. While there, we must have shopped in every antiquarian bookstore in the city (in those days, there were many). I had been astounded to find a first edition of *Surprised by Joy* for only thirty-five pounds, about fifty dollars at the then exchange rate. Nelle was equally amazed when we told her. The clerk had explained that the bargain basement price resulted from growing secularization of England and that Lewis had become more popular in the U.S. than in his own country. I added that I also had purchased a first edition of Lewis's BBC wartime lectures. She quickly reminded me that the title was *Mere Christianity*. This conversation occurred eighteen months before her death, at the beginning of persistent media reports of her dementia. The day she died, she was still plowing through that massive anthology.

While rereading *Surprised by Joy* after her death, I found the meaning of what at the time had struck me as a cryptic sentence: Lewis was "the greatest Christian apologist since St. Augustine's *Confessions*." Of course, that meant that she had read St. Augustine's *Confessions*. But her exclamation was more complex than that. It summarized an important concept of Christianity, the relationship of belief to ethics. Lewis began the final chapter of his book by quoting in both Latin and English a passage from *Confessions*: "For it is one thing to see the land of peace from a wooded ridge . . . and another to tread the road that leads to it."

LEWIS'S FAMOUS THEOLOGICAL LECTURES for the BBC during the darkest days of World War II were grounded in a specific biblical cycle: innocence; temptation; sin; alienation; confrontation; repentance; forgiveness; reconciliation. Written a decade after his lectures and their publication in *Mere Christianity*, *Go Set a Watchman* transferred Lewis's theology from its setting in England amidst global violence to Maycomb, Alabama. Was America capable of repenting of its "original sin" of racism? How could a nation do so if even the fictional hero Atticus Finch could not surmount his racist culture?

In *Mockingbird*, innocence is represented by the instinctive sense of fairness often found in children, while moral ambiguity and hypocrisy dominate the adult world of churches, courtrooms, and juries. Perhaps that explains why Lee has Dill decide that he doesn't want to grow up. Or why Atticus Finch cynically describes the all-white jury verdict of guilty as "just as much Maycomb County as missionary teas." The children learn authentic

Christianity and the ideals of American justice from Calpurnia, from her preacher in their church, and in the "colored balcony" of the courthouse listening to the conflicting testimony in the Tom Robinson trial.

In her novels, Harper Lee described a flawed, fallen, imperfect world, yet one not beyond redemption. By doing so, she avoided the nihilism and despair of much modern fiction. For every hypocritical Aunt Alexandra, there is an authentic Christian such as Maudie Atkinson. And at his best, Atticus's admonition against judging a person "until you walk around in his shoes" is a modern paraphrase of Matthew 7:1 from the Sermon on the Mount.

Lutheran theologian Frederick Buechner distinguishes between "religion" books and "religious" books. "Religion" books about ministers, priests, churches, cathedrals, sacraments, rituals, and beliefs explore human institutions. "Religious" books such as C. S. Lewis's *Chronicles of Narnia* and J. R. R. Tolkien's *Lord of the Rings* brilliantly incorporate Christian mythology. I insisted to Nelle that by Buechner's definition, her novels are "religious." She refused to participate in personal theological speculation.

Cerebral theology was less interesting to her than Methodist hymnody. One springtime afternoon, a bird landed on the bird feeder outside her window. By then, she recognized only shapes of objects and asked Dartie what kind of bird it was. Dartie—a serious "birder" whose table looking out onto our feeder in the woods was piled high with photographic books of feathery creatures—identified Nelle's visitor as a female house sparrow, at which point Nelle broke into song: "I sing because I'm happy; I sing because I'm free. His eye is on the sparrow and I know he watches me." We added our voices on the next verse, reviving our impromptu trio, Nelle singing melody, Dartie alto, and me bass. I was unanimously acknowledged to be the worst singer.

Evidence that this incident was no fluke came three years later. I was summarizing a forum on ABC Radio Australia, that nation's public radio system. When Australians selected *Mockingbird* as their favorite novel by an American, I was asked to participate in the discussion. I thought Nelle would be interested in the varying points of view, but she interrupted my story by singing several stanzas of "Waltzing Matilda" loudly and well.

I was so impressed that I walked over to her wheelchair and kissed her on the cheek. She was startled. And after considering what I had done, I was too. The three of us sat in silence for a few seconds. Nelle broke the spell by exclaiming, "I like being kissed by a man with a mustache!" I could feel my ears turning red as the blood flowed to them. Dartie broke another long pause: "It's like going through brambles on the way to a picnic. Once you arrive, it's lots of fun." I blushed even more. Nelle howled with laughter. Dartie just smiled. That day we knew we had entered a new and more intimate stage of friendship.

A year later, I read a letter-to-the-editor in the *Birmingham News* written by a young woman who had shared an awards ceremony with Nelle at the University of Alabama decades earlier. Also a resident of New York City, she recognized Nelle when they were waiting to board a city bus. They exchanged greetings, after which Nelle invited her to lunch. She led the way to a fashionable Manhattan restaurant. The woman was astounded at how friendly and talkative Nelle was, even inquiring about her profession. She replied that she composed and recorded "new Christian music." Never one to conceal her opinions about anything, Nelle said she did not like that kind of music. Embarrassed, the woman added that she also recorded traditional hymns such as "Leaning on the Everlasting Arms." There, in the trendy Manhattan restaurant filled with a lunchtime audience not accustomed to entertainment, Nelle broke into a solo *a cappella* rendition of the old gospel hymn. Dartie and I fantasized about how the New York lunch crowd processed that.

Chapter 5

An American Dilemma: Class and Race

FOR MIDDLE-CLASS WHITE WOMEN COMING OF AGE IN THE DEEP South during the first third of the twentieth century, Nelle and her sisters developed complicated, nuanced attitudes about class and race. When they thought about class at all, they tended to personalize the concept. On learning about the Flynts' family origins in the Appalachian foothills of northeast Alabama, the Lees detached that information entirely from our university educations, teaching careers, and love of literature, theater, and history. In short, our personal biographies were surprising but not important.

Although Nelle briefly wrestled with class relationships in print, she sometimes misinterpreted them, as demonstrated by one of her few misreadings of Alabama history. Her character, Jean Louise Finch ("Scout") believed that her novice twenty-one-year-old first-grade teacher, the prim and proper Miss Caroline Fisher from Winston County, could not understand poor white children such as Walter Cunningham. Actually, few young teachers would have better understood a poor white child than one from mountainous, isolated, poor, white northwest Alabama. Winston County contained few cotton plantations or African

Americans and was more like fictional Maycomb County's "Old Sarum." Winston County had strongly opposed secession, and most of its men who chose to fight in the war that came did so in the blue uniforms of the Union Army.

As a consequence, Winston was the scene of atrocities by both sides in a civil war within the Civil War. Following the war, Winston County maintained its insurgent tradition, voting as Lincoln Republicans until the Great Depression, in a state that had always voted Democrat. Any teacher from the county would have understood young Walter Cunningham's world much better than a teacher who came of age in Monroe County. The Cunninghams' experiences with "entailment" (loss of land) and debts settled with croker sacks of hickory nuts, smilax, holly, and turnip greens would have been no surprise to Miss Caroline. Although Walter's father was so poor he could not afford shoes for his son, Lee describes him as so proud he was willing to starve if necessary to "vote as he pleased." That was a perfect description of my Republican cousin who lived in Winston County.

Although Nelle veered off course occasionally about class in *Mockingbird*, she demonstrated keen insights into the 1901 Alabama constitution that disfranchised nearly all blacks and most poor whites such as our grandparents. That constitution, which continues to misgovern the state, raised every barrier possible to suppress poor folks' voting. As she wrote, it stands as a shabby memorial to the coalition of south Alabama planters and Birmingham industrialists who were much too shrewd to leave the political fate of the state in the hands of people like the poor white Cunninghams. By the 1930s, the constitution, which Nelle's father fervently supported in the state legislature, disfranchised more than half the adult population of the state. Tenant farmers, such as Dartie's and my grandfathers, tended 70 percent of the state's cotton plantations and 65 percent of all farms. Assuming other tenant families had similar fertility rates (my father was one of eight children, his mother one of eighteen), the 35,000 white tenant families and 33,000 black renters comprised more than a quarter of Alabama's total population.

Nelle did portray accurately the state's class pyramid. Its apex consisted of planters and urban businessmen/industrialists. Some planters such as the kindly Link Dees in *Mockingbird* provided work for black men such as Tom Robinson who tended equipment and mended fences after an accident that cost the use of an arm. Most planters assumed no such responsibility. Families such as the Cunninghams farmed marginal land and often lost even that during depressions.

Black farm laborers such as Tom Robinson might occupy the lowest rung on the agricultural ladder, but Robert E. Lee Ewell descended even lower in the opinion of both whites and blacks. He was poor but not proud, living next to the garbage dump and adjacent to the town's African American neighborhood. Nelle described his family as welfare recipients, "guests of the county in prosperity and depression."

I confirmed the accuracy of Nelle's class analysis one afternoon in the state archives while examining public welfare records for 1935. Of the 1,600 children surveyed, 67 percent suffered from physical defects such as malnutrition, pellagra, hookworm, rickets, and venereal disease. Incest by the woefully misnamed Robert E. Lee Ewell was not unknown among such families. I once joked to Nelle that my research into Alabama's class system had provided the historical platform on which she had constructed her novel. She rebutted that her novel came before my books.

That provoked a discussion about why nearly a century after the setting of *Mockingbird* Americans persisted in using tropes such as "deserving" and "undeserving" poor, "poor white trash," and "trailer trash" as shorthand for discussions of class. I also mentioned the irony of appropriating the family name of the "poor but proud" Cunninghams from her own mother, Frances Cunningham Finch Lee, thereby either bestowing dignity upon them or satirizing her.

THE SUBJECT OF RACE is even more contentious than class. As a Christian without the superficial piety that too often accompanies such conviction, Alice Lee had quietly and gradually nudged Monroeville beyond racial separatism. It helped that Lee and the African American Tucker family were educational and personal friends. When their daughter, Cynthia Tucker, longtime journalist at the *Atlanta Journal-Constitution*, won a Pulitzer Prize for her editorials about race in America, the entire town could boast that so small a place had produced two Pulitzer winners. Tucker's father had not only been a school principal in Monroe County, he earned extra income as a golf caddy for Nelle's father. Tucker's mother was a beloved schoolteacher and civic leader.

Alice Lee combined her expertise in tax law with her pivotal leadership of the Methodist Church, where she taught the influential men's Sunday school class. Although inclined by nature to avoid controversy, she instructed ushers to seat any African Americans who sought to worship there during the contentious 1960s, when such action was nearly unheard of in Alabama's Black Belt.

She was also the person who invited me to present my iconoclastic interpretation of race, class, gender, and the Bible to a Methodist women's conference.

Louise and Nelle told us stories about family "servants" whose roles in raising children of an aging father and bipolar mother sometimes absent or too depressed to manage household chores were equally revealing. Nelle depicted the fictional Calpurnia as stern and nurturing in *Mockingbird* but confrontational, sullen, and strident in *Watchman*. She explained that the character was a composite of all their cooks and maids.

Whatever the source of their father's racial myopia—Confederate ancestors, upbringing, politics, or white evangelical emphasis on personal conversion rather than social justice—his three daughters moved beyond the boundaries of Monroeville's racial culture in their own ways and at different speeds. So did he, according to Ed Conner, who speculates that Nelle allowed Coley Lee to read *Watchman* during his last years, and that manuscript, together with the fame of *Mockingbird*, led to their reconciliation.

One of Louise's dearest friends in Eufaula often traveled with her to attend plays and concerts in nearby Columbus, Georgia. But in the late 1960s, when Louise continued to support public schools after most white parents enrolled their children in a new segregated private academy, their friendship waned. When Louise ventured even further, collaborating with a progressive mayor and other public officials in support of a tax increase for public schools, and serving on a biracial community affairs committee, even inviting an African American member to her home for coffee, she lost more friends. We speculated that her shrinking social circle may have opened her home and heart to us. If so, it was Eufaula's loss and our good fortune.

Opinions about Harper Lee's views on race vary. In the historical context of the 1930s–1950s, she was progressive by Alabama and Southern standards. During a 1963 interview, Lee repeated a familiar theme of proportionality when writing about small towns in the South: There was not a "lynching before every breakfast." "I think that Southerners react with the same kind of horror that other people do about the injustice in their land."

Unfortunately, she was too optimistic about the South's capacity to maintain law and order, predicting that whites in Mississippi were so stunned by a recent racial murder that they would not allow repetition of such an atrocity. Pressed by the reporter who asked her opinion of Mississippi Governor Ross Barnett, who had defied a federal court order to integrate the University of Mississippi, she deferred to the court system: "I presume the gentleman is innocent until proven guilty. But I presume he will be proven guilty. I think he was wrong."

Although she did not endorse the 1961 Freedom Rides led by fellow Alabamian John Lewis because the civil rights direct actions "flouted state laws," she did affirm Dr. Martin Luther King Jr. and the NAACP for challenging segregation in "exactly the right way," through federal courts. She predicted that white people in the South "may not like it, but they will respect it." At least in the Deep South, that prophecy proved too hopeful.

When a different reporter pressed her whether *Mockingbird* was an "indictment against a group in society," she chose a different phrase to explain her purpose: "The book is not an indictment so much as a plea for something, a reminder to people at home."

When pressed further whether her characters in *Mockingbird* were based on real people in Monroeville, she coyly replied: "No, but the people at home think so."

ALABAMA IS OFTEN STEREOTYPED, seldom carefully studied, and even less frequently understood for its significant minority of New Deal liberals and racial iconoclasts. Nonetheless, progressive racial ideas often resulted in a politician's defeat or a minister's dismissal. Nelle's father was primarily responsible for removing a "liberal" pastor of Monroeville's Methodist Church who preached social justice too much and repentance from sin too little. Alice Lee also acquiesced in the transfer. By the time the family related the story to us, it was the minister's poor preaching, not his over-emphasis on social justice, that resulted in his replacement.

One hero we shared with Harper Lee was Judge James Edwin Horton Jr., of Decatur, Alabama. In March 1933, he presided at the second trial of the "Scottsboro boys," nine black youths falsely accused of raping two white women, all illegally riding a freight train near Scottsboro, Alabama. Despite the best efforts of their attorney—whose Judaism, New York residence, and support by the American Communist Party did their cause no good in Alabama—the all-white male jury unanimously voted the death penalty for all of them. Judge Horton rejected the verdict based on conflicting medical evidence and agreed to a defense motion for a new trial. In the following election, Horton was defeated and never held public office again.

By the late 1940s when Nelle was studying law, the innocence of the Scottsboro boys was assumed by most of her professors, and the state parole board was poised to free the remaining convicts.

Rumors circulated that Nelle once considered writing a novel about the case.

When Nelle was a freshman in college in 1944, the Reverend Arthur M. Carlton, a twenty-five-year-old second-generation Methodist minister was assigned his first pastorate in a small south Alabama town after graduating from Duke University's divinity school. While drinking coffee one morning in the local drug store, he overheard a conspiracy to lynch an African American being held in jail. He reported the plot to the sheriff, and a deputy placed the man in a police car and raced out of town followed by Reverend Carlton, who used his vehicle to block the lynch mob following behind. After news of the chase spread, Klansmen burned a cross in front of the Methodist parsonage. The presiding Methodist bishop reassigned the courageous young pastor to a more progressive urban congregation.

During the reign of apartheid, it did not require a great deal of unconventional thinking to label someone a dangerous radical. She never specifically mentioned such fears, but perhaps this closing of the collective Alabama mind, or at least its tongue, played a role in Nelle's abandonment of Alabama for New York City. If so, history played a trick on her. In 1954 the U.S. Supreme Court directed the first blow at segregated public schools in *Brown v. Board of Education*. The following year, Rosa Parks was arrested for refusing to obey segregation laws on a city bus, triggering the celebrated Montgomery Bus Boycott. Over the next decade, sit-ins, Freedom Rides, street protests, and voter registration campaigns, featuring the powerful voices and examples of black leaders like Martin Luther King Jr. and John Lewis, prodded President Lyndon B. Johnson to send Congress the 1964 Civil Rights Act and the 1965 Voting Rights Act.

Newly returned to Samford University, my alma mater in Birmingham in 1965, I considered John Lewis one of my heroes. Decades later I voted for his long overdue election to the Alabama Academy of Honor, and we had a brief conversation about our divergent careers.

In the shifting sands of literary and historical consciousness, critics began writing that the fictional Atticus Finch and even Harper Lee were, if not complicit in resisting racial change, at best gradualists. Publication in 2015 of *Go Set a Watchman* complicated that interpretation by moving the chronology of Atticus's life from the economic devastation of the 1930s (*Mockingbird*) to the racially toxic 1950s (*Watchman*), from New Deal Alabama governors and congressmen to George C. Wallace and his cronies. Although the state regrettably had always tolerated them, racial atrocities and white supremacist rhetoric escalated during the Wallace years.

My modest contribution to the resistance movement was faculty sponsorship of the Young Democrats chapter at Samford University and a tutoring program in Homewood's majority-black Rosedale community. Many male heads-of-family there were skilled middle-class steel workers or other industrial employees with stable families who took pride in their local high school. Unfortunately, teachers in Alabama's black schools had few resources such as microscopes, advanced science, or foreign language classes. After passage of the Voting Rights Act, we also organized a voter registration drive. Our efforts in 1966 were timid compared to John Lewis's, but only three years earlier "Dynamite" Robert "Bob" Chambliss and three of his Ku Klux

Klan henchmen had murdered four black girls at the Sixteenth Street Baptist Church in downtown Birmingham. The bombers were not identified until November 1977 after our family moved to Auburn. I never mentioned to that courageous band of white Samford students during our voter registration drive leading up to the 1968 presidential election that somewhere in the moral slums of Birmingham those mass murderers still lurked. I think they all knew it anyway.

When I drove a black woman in her eighties or nineties to register, she sported a fine dress crowned by a Sunday hat that Dartie would have lusted for. Her high heels were ancient but sturdy. When I returned to Rosedale to take her to vote, the clerk asked her to write her name on the voter list. Embarrassed, she explained that she could not read or write. It was our transition into the new world aborning, so the clerk said something stupid: "Well, if you can't read or write, how do you intend to vote?" After a short pause for a three-way reflection, I explained that I would go inside the booth with her, read the names, and she would pull the lever. I could not do that, the clerk said loudly as a long line of white voters behind me began to grumble. Temper rising, I said that the clerk obviously had not read the 1965 Voting Rights Act which provided for such a situation. And, for emphasis, I added that if the State of Alabama had distributed proportional revenue to the black population during this woman's youth, we would not be having this conversation. That is when the clerk threatened to have me arrested. Knowing as I did that the U.S. Justice Department had flooded Alabama and Mississippi with monitors for this first truly interracial U.S. election since Reconstruction, with voice trembling, I told the clerk that I would probably be out of the Homewood jail before she exited a federal penitentiary. That seemed to have a calming effect, and the conversation ended when she said, "Well, I don't like this," while handing the voter the list, which she signed with an "X" next to which I wrote her name. We marched into the booth, I read the names, she pulled the lever, and I swear she exited the precinct inches taller than when she arrived. Nelle loved the story, especially the ending, when I speculated about how some of her Northern critics might have handled that confrontation in Birmingham four years after white terrorists who were still at large had murdered four black children. But that was my rant. She never tried to explain her depiction of her father in *Watchman* or *Mockingbird*.

SHORTLY AFTER *Mockingbird* WAS published, Nelle wrote a spirited defense of Ralph Ellison, who had attended Alabama's Tuskegee Institute for a few years before he took flight to Harlem. In 1953 he won the National Book Award for his novel, *Invisible Man*, loosely based on what he perceived as the gradualism and moral compromises made by Tuskegee's president Booker T. Washington. Many whites considered the novel a radical expression of the Harlem Renaissance.

Denunciations soon came from the opposite ideological direction as well. In "A Very Stern Discipline," an interview with Ellison published in 1967, he mobilized American literature from Mark Twain to Richard Wright to illustrate how writers had dealt with race in America. His brilliant interview reignited a long-standing feud. During the 1930s, leftist black writers such as Richard Wright and Langston Hughes had heaped criticism on the writings of Alabama native Zora Neale Hurston, whose anthropological/folklorist fiction was less class-oriented than stridently feminist. Ellison's novel stirred the kettle to a new froth as some black critics dismissed him as a one-book phenomenon, provoking a rebuttal from Harper Lee in a letter-to-the-editor of *Harper's* magazine in May 1971.

> When Ralph Ellison tackles the sacred cows of literary criticism [in his interview] his fellow novelists react with unholy joy. When he speaks of his country he makes every thinking citizen share his deep love and concern. When he demands his right to his own identity and unique gifts, he demands the same right for all of us. If he grinds any axe, it is the axe of individual excellence.
>
> Seldom in this age do we find a writer whose clear-headedness is equal to his title. We are more fortunate than we deserve in having one of our very own—home-grown and utterly American. "A Very Stern Discipline" is vintage Ellison.

I read Nelle's own grievances in her letter. Like Ellison, she loved her country, which required her to challenge readers to think seriously about race. By inference, she defended her own Southern female identity and "unique gifts." If she ground an axe, it was the axe of prodigious work and "individual excellence." As much as Ellison, she considered herself "home-grown and utterly American." In a sense, her 1971 defense of Ellison could have been her own posthumous rebuttal to twenty-first-century literary critics and presentist historians who considered her narrative in *Mockingbird* too accommodationist to a racist father and culture.

Nelle's friendships with Lyndon and Lady Bird Johnson,

arguably architects of the most liberal reform agenda in American presidential history, bolstered her credentials on race. LBJ had awarded Ellison the Presidential Medal of Freedom in 1969, and Ronald Reagan gave him the Medal of the Arts sixteen years later. George W. Bush awarded Harper Lee the Presidential Medal of Freedom in 2007, and Barack Obama awarded her the National Medal of the Arts in 2010.

One afternoon I summarized these stories for her and suggested that *Invisible Man* and *To Kill a Mockingbird* (*Watchman* was not yet known) were both "race novels" written during the era of desegregation, white grievance, and massive resistance. She smiled but did not comment about my hypothesis nor the irony of both writers receiving awards from presidents of opposing parties.

IN SOME WAYS HER friendships provided a better insight into her views on race. Although her relationship with the Johnsons was most notable, her close friends were racial progressives. Diane McWhorter, like Nelle, departed Alabama for New York City. Daughter of a socially prominent and wealthy family in one of America's richest suburbs, the dissonance between the world from which McWhorter came and the one to which she went was as revealing as her Pulitzer-winning memoir, *Carry Me Home: Birmingham, Alabama: The Climactic Battle of the Civil Rights Movement*. The book described similarities between the famous Montgomery Bus Boycott in 1956 and the nearly forgotten Birmingham business boycott that launched the "Birmingham Movement" in 1963.

Seen in historical rather than literary perspective, Nelle's two novels and McWhorter's memoir are of a single piece. Rather than ambivalent and timid hints that something might be amiss in America, Nelle's *Mockingbird* and *Watchman* and McWhorter's *Carry Me Home*, in the words of Flannery O'Connor, "shout" and "draw large and startling figures" to name America's "original sin."

All three Lee sisters seemed intuitively to understand that America was changing and that Alabama possessed an almost Biblical relevance to the nation's racial dilemma. Governor George Wallace's successful forays into America's midwestern heartland in 1968 and 1972—which foreshadowed Donald Trump's victory there in 2016 and near-win in 2020—demonstrated that Alabama might not be able to elect a native-born bigot to the presidency but could certainly help elect a surrogate from New York City. I have no doubt about Nelle's opinion of Trump thanks to a story her nephew Ed Conner told me. While he was visiting her in New York City, she told him that Trump was a vulgar, loudmouth "narcissistic tycoon and a horrible person" who liked to name everything after himself.

Given Nelle's denunciation of her father figure's cultural racism in *Watchman* and her much more nuanced depiction of him in *Mockingbird*, we were surprised that increasingly both novels were portrayed not in the historical context of their own time but in the shadow of "Black Lives Matter" from 2013. Whereas the national reaction to *Mockingbird* was celebratory and the Southern reaction cautious and sometimes negative, by 2021 her own people had enshrined her while *Mockingbird* was being banned in California and Minnesota public schools.

She received one of her favorite honors, the Birmingham Pledge Lifetime Achievement Award, in September 2006 only months before her stroke. The event was remarkable both for venue and audience. James E. Rotch, a prominent Birmingham attorney appalled by the city's racist past, established the Birmingham Pledge Foundation. Mainly symbolic and aspirational, its pledge tried to achieve racial justice and community unity by moral suasion and personal example:

> I believe that every person has worth as an individual.
>
> I believe that every person is entitled to dignity and respect, regardless of race or color.
>
> I believe that every thought and every act of racial prejudice is harmful; if it is my thought or act, then it is harmful to me as well as others.
>
> Therefore, from this day forward I will strive daily to eliminate racial prejudice from my thoughts and actions.
>
> I will discourage racial prejudice by others at every opportunity.
>
> I will treat all people with dignity and respect; and I will strive daily to honor this pledge, knowing that the world will be a better place because of my effort.

Although sincere and elemental if America is ever to surmount its racist past, the pledge was too long to memorize like the Boy Scout oath, and it was an easy target for satire from both racists and African Americans who grew up in Police Commissioner Bull Connor's Birmingham. What really changed the city was federal civil rights legislation during the Johnson administration, vigorous prosecution by the U.S. Justice Department, and tough enforcement by federal judges. The city's business leaders also experienced an epiphany when they stared into the abyss of local black resistance, national economic boycotts, white flight to the suburbs, changing racial demographics, and the impending black takeover of city government.

Given the inevitability of change, I was surprised that the famously reclusive novelist agreed to accept the award knowing as I did what was in store for her: a private fundraiser where well-heeled people would shell out money in order to tell friends they had met the elusive writer; long lines of well-wishers who would pay for a seat in the cavernous Alys Stephens Performing Arts Center of the University of Alabama in Birmingham; and business and community leaders who believed an elixir such as the Birmingham Pledge and Harper Lee were just the tonic an ailing city needed to mend its frayed national reputation. Her consent to subject herself to such public exposure expressed almost better than anything she wrote which side of America's racial divide she favored.

MEANWHILE, I HAD PLANNED a surprise for her. For months I had been working with a unique theatrical venture. Pat Yates, one of those amazing teachers who transform students' lives, directed the theater program at elite Mountain Brook High School. The school regularly sent many of its graduates to Ivy League universities. Of course, all the students had read *To Kill a Mockingbird* in middle school. The problem was the school had few black students, and even those tended to be more bookish or athletic than theatrical or musical. To produce the play, *Mockingbird*, she would need musically talented black high schoolers. Her solution was Patsy Houze, choral director at all-black Fairfield Industrial High School, located in a declining steel mill suburb west of

Birmingham. To say that the two schools and student bodies differed in background, race, income, residence, and opportunity is a vast understatement.

When Yates called to ask if I would meet in Fairfield with the two groups to discuss Harper Lee and her novel, I welcomed the opportunity. I had time to chat with the Fairfield students before the Mountain Brook contingent arrived, although "chat" is a poor choice of words: it was more my monologue. No comments or questions from them. When the Mountain Brook students arrived, they trekked to the opposite side of the room. Having just met, they were already mirroring racial separation.

I began the session with the most obvious question: "What is the theme of *To Kill a Mockingbird*?" The silence seemed to last longer than the creation of the universe. Finally, more from wanting the nightmare to end than anything else, a black student said: "Underneath our skin we are all the same! Don't judge somebody until you walk around in his shoes." "Exactly!" I shouted in relief.

Having broken the ice, we proceeded to a fruitful discussion of apartheid, racial justice, and Judeo-Christian ethics. I thought the first meeting was a bit early in the tutorial to mention incest, alleged rape, and a young white woman's lust for a strong, hard-working black man. As roles were assigned, rehearsals began, and musically gifted black students encountered the technological miracles of a wealthy white school funded by the highest local property taxes in Alabama. But we all marveled at the variety of talents available in the mixed cast and even more at their rapidly developing friendships.

We had told Nelle about the forthcoming play but did not expect the cast to appear for the reception at the Alys Stephens

Center the night of her award. When we arrived, Dartie and I encountered Nelle's fans in a long line stretching from where she stood greeting them one by one, all the way to the entrance of the auditorium. She was obviously exhausted from standing, shaking hands, and trying to hear people over the cacophony. When our eyes met, hers flashed a familiar "Get me out of here!" When I looked at the long line, I could think of no solution. But in my simple theology, God sometimes provides a way. Suddenly in came the entire *Mockingbird* cast dressed as their characters. I walked to the students and told them to follow me, broke in line, and asked Nelle to sit on the couch behind her as the students spread out around her. "Thank God!" she muttered much too audibly for my comfort as the director of this incivility and collapsed onto the couch.

Dartie and I agreed that the following quarter-hour observing her interaction with the students was one of our finest times with her. She laughed. She complimented their costumes and makeup. She paid attention to their stories, characters, and cast-mates.

Meanwhile, if angry stares could kill, I would have been dead a hundred times over. Thankfully, Jim Rotch rescued me, escorting us to the front of the auditorium where I had been recruited to speak briefly. Aware of her obsession with privacy, I had decided to speak only about her book, especially emphasizing how Atticus Finch incorporated some of the themes of the Birmingham Pledge. Nelle was close enough to me and the sound system was sufficiently loud for her to hear every word.

Afterwards, she announced: "That is going to be my eulogy. I want you to deliver it. Don't change a word. And I don't want any other preachers." At the time, I was not sure whether she didn't know I was an ordained minister or had read enough of my books to decide it really didn't make any difference. Or, perhaps she had concluded I was not enough of a preacher to matter. The next week she sent a letter confirming the "request," which more resembled a command performance, complete with a copy to Alice and her nephew, Hank Conner. She also complained that the *Birmingham News* had not printed my entire tribute to her because it was too long.

In January 2007, Nelle again dressed elegantly and traveled to Montgomery, the first capital of the Confederacy, for another award. This occasion coincided with an encore performance of *Mockingbird* by the mixed-race troupe of teenagers before a packed theater of Alabama's political, social, and business elites. After the performance, which she skipped while talking with us, a crescendo of ovations and calls for "Author! Author!" brought her on stage to receive accolades from cast and audience. She grinned from ear to ear and flashed a smile for the ages, but did not speak even a word.

She invited us, our son Sean, and daughter-in-law Shannon to Monroeville for a visit before she returned to New York City. That day at Alice's house Nelle was witty, ebullient, thoughtful, and uncharacteristically talkative. Before she returned to New York, we drove down once more and she was equally upbeat.

Two months later, on March 17, 2007, she suffered a stroke. The woman who returned to Alabama would be quite different from the one who left the state in 1949, not only physically but psychologically. The recent awards had persuaded her that a simple pledge of fairness, decency, and racial justice no longer disqualified a writer from the state's love and pride. If we had failed to convince her of that, the mixed-race cast, thunderous ovations, and overflow crowds in Birmingham and Montgomery had persuaded her that a prophet need not be without honor in her own state, and that Alabama was not the same place she had left sixty years earlier. She told us that the Birmingham Pledge day was "the best day of my life."

AWAY FROM THE CROWDS, we observed more intimate glimpses of Alabama's racial transition. Marsilla Harrington, a middle-aged Monroeville African American woman, was caregiver for Alice Lee until her death. When we visited Alice in the nursing home, Marsilla announced our presence, summarized Alice's capacity to hear and understand us, and mentioned her difficulty speaking. Then she retired into silence while we talked to Alice.

After Alice's death, Marcilla was one of several caregivers for Nelle, mirroring her earlier pattern: mostly silent but with facial expressions that made it clear that she heard and understood every word. Dartie included the caregivers in the candy, cookies, pies, and cakes we brought.

One day I told Nelle and Marsilla about a forthcoming trip to the Library of Congress to participate in an awards ceremony for the recipient of the Harper Lee Prize in Legal Fiction sponsored by the University of Alabama Law School and the American Bar Association. I had been chosen as a juror for the 2015 prize and a panelist for the ensuing discussion of the book. Our unanimous choice was Deborah Johnston, the first African American recipient of the prize. Nelle was delighted, so I asked her and Marsilla if they wanted copies of the winning novel. Nelle declined because of her rapidly deteriorating vision, but her caregiver seemed delighted. While she was tending Alice, I had given Marsilla a copy of Zora Neale Hurston's *Their Eyes Were Watching God*, one of my favorite novels. She loved the book and shared it with many friends who also liked it.

When I returned from Washington, I gave Marsilla an inscribed copy of Johnston's *The Secret of Magic,* and she seemed transformed as she read and reread Deborah's inscription to her. She talked with us, laughed, and two months later at Christmas told me she had finished the book and loved it.

Following that visit, Marsilla treated us more as friends than visitors, explaining in a whisper one afternoon when we arrived, that Nelle did not feel well, had skipped lunch, and needed to sleep. We returned home sad to have missed a day with Nelle but pleased she had so fine a caregiver. We knew that she would spend her last days with caregivers who genuinely cared for her.

Shortly thereafter, I was reading Gerald Early's essay on young adult fiction written in the 1960s that discussed racial terms Nelle had used in *Mockingbird*. He lumped them into a literary category of "New Southern Gothic" writing: "Even in a world where nature is racialized and we have a 'nigger snowman,' we know that the white snow falls upon the black earth. There they become one, and different from what they were separately." I counted the ways this was true in Southern history: music, religion, folklore, art, fishing, hunting, interracial marriages. And the ways it was not: legal justice, jobs, the economy, education, healthcare, incarceration rates.

People as diverse as former President Bill Clinton, Democratic strategist James Carville, attorneys and best-selling novelists Scott Turow and John Grisham, Morris Dees (founder of the Southern

Poverty Law Center), and Justin Skilton (president of the Wisconsin Bar Association cited the fictional Atticus Finch as important in their decisions to study law and advocate for greater justice in America. That fact ought to mean something to the sometimes ahistorical generation that seemed to believe that hardly anything before "Black Lives Matter" actually mattered. Many important American reform movements constructed their passion upon the premise that intractable injustice could be swept away in one great torrent of emotional engagement, energy, and legislation. Serious historians and theologians of the American past mostly have concluded that change occurs by convulsive fits and starts rather than by sustained conquest of human tendencies that are rooted in narcissism, materialism, and injustice.

Not surprisingly, the obvious model for my hypothesis was the nation's first African American president, Barack Obama. He understood better than most Americans how many steep and perilous cultural and historical mountains of resistance to change exist in America. I noticed early in his presidency that he often quoted or paraphrased Atticus Finch without identifying his source. When speaking in Tel Aviv in 2013, he implored Jewish university students to try harder to understand Muslim Palestinians. With his signature combination of empathy and urgency, he entreated them to: "Put yourselves in their shoes. Look at things through their eyes." I thought at the time that he was paraphrasing Atticus Finch. One evening as I was watching PBS NewsHour on a day when nothing of great importance happened, a cameo moment showed Barack Obama on vacation. He was emerging from a bookstore with a package. The reporter shouted past a cordon of Secret Service agents, "Mr. President, what did you buy?" After a moment's hesitation, Obama answered: "A copy of *To Kill a Mockingbird* for Malia's birthday."

So frequently did such references occur that I began to record them. I need not have bothered because Spencer Kornhaber had noticed the same pattern, which he described in a thoughtful essay in *The Atlantic* entitled "Obama's Ingenious Mention of Atticus Finch." He focused on the literary flaws of Atticus Finch revealed in *Go Set a Watchman* by Atticus's own daughter as well as by A. C. Lee's real-life compromises as revealed by historians. He noted that Obama had come under similar scrutiny from the Democratic left for his own compromises and gradualism. Kornhaber ended his essay by focusing on Obama's farewell address to packed throngs in Chicago on his last day in office. I had listened to that same passionate speech, then copied the *New York Times* account in my journal:

> If our democracy is to work in this increasingly diverse nation, each one of us must heed the advice of one of the greatest characters in American fiction, Atticus Finch: "You never really understand a person until you consider things from his point of view . . . until you climb into his skin and walk around in it."

As Kornhaber noted, the nation's first black president sounded a good deal like Atticus Finch even after quoting him: "Blacks and other minorities" should be "tying our own stereotypes for justice to the challenges that a lot of people in the country face," including "the middle-aged white man who's seen his world upended by economic, cultural, and technological change." Asking his admirers to understand disgruntled white men on the eve of Donald

Trump's presidency must have seemed as serious a betrayal of his ideals as Nelle's portrayal of her father in *Watchman*.

Kornhaber perceptively concluded that Obama was extolling neither a flawed literary creation nor racist white working-class grievances: "He was calling on America to ensure that the best version of itself, and the best version of its heroes, reemerge."

Chapter 6

New York, New York

JANE AUSTEN COMPOSED AT LEAST ONE SENTENCE WITH WHICH Harper Lee vigorously disagreed: "Ah, there is nothing like staying home for real comfort." Nelle considered the day she caught a train to New York City one of the happiest in her life. She never expressed regrets about leaving her family, law school, or Alabama. In New York City she met Texas native Maurice Crain who would become her literary agent, and Tay Hohoff, her editor.

No one encouraged her move more fervently than childhood friend Truman Capote. Born in New Orleans in 1924 two years before Nelle, Capote lived for months at a time with his Faulk aunts and uncle in a rambling house separated from the Lees' by a four-foot-high stone wall. He lived there full-time 1930–32 while his divorced mother established a new life and family in New York City. After rejoining her and his new stepfather, he regularly returned to Monroeville for visits, even writing his first book in a cabin behind his cousin's farmhouse.

The Faulks were essentially a dysfunctional family. Its males especially tended to disappear into wars or domestic irresponsibility. On a July 4th afternoon, Nelle described them to us in a metaphor: "Both sides of Truman's family fled from the truth like Dracula fled from the cross. And Truman," she added for emphasis, was also "inclined to shade the truth." During that visit, we chatted for a while about his mother, Lillie Mae, and her sisters, Mary Ida and Lucille. I asked which she liked best: "I guess Lucille," she laughed, "because she was deaf."

Dartie and I had to process her nonchalance about Truman's family within the context of his colossal ego, self-destructive adult life, and their alienation in the 1960s. During their childhoods, however, they were virtually inseparable whenever he was in Monroeville.

Her real favorite among the Faulk women was Sook, who lived in the house next door with two sisters and a brother, plus whichever kin showed up like some stray dog wandering lost in the world. She described Sook as poorly educated and a faithful Baptist except when sampling moonshine whiskey while making fruitcakes at Christmas. Nelle said Sook's cakes were as fine as Monroeville folklore claimed. Dartie interrupted to tell her that for Christmas a friend had given her a copy of *Sook's Cookbook: Memories and Traditional Receipts from the Deep South*. Nelle broke into laughter, proclaiming, "Sook never put a meal on the table in her life. But she could make fruitcakes. Sook was all innocence and completely devoted to Truman. And she was the only person Truman really loved. He loved her to the end."

I replied that "A Christmas Memory," the story of Truman's and Sook's mutual affection, was our favorite short story. Nelle described it as "Truman's love letter to Sook."

From there she moved into a discussion of Truman's literary legacy, especially *Other Voices, Other Rooms* and *The Grass Harp*, books about his childhood which provide clues to his and Nelle's friendship.

As a child, Truman boasted that he had total recall, and he certainly was precocious. Nelle remembered that he helped inspire Thelma Dees to conduct an informal summer school for bright Monroeville youngsters with too much time on their hands. She remembered seven-year-old Truman telling Dees one day that something she told the students was "fascinating," "a word," she laughed, "nearly as big as he was."

Nelle defended Truman in playground brawls, and when not in school they roamed the town and out into the countryside seeking adventure. I asked why boys bullied Truman. She answered, "Because he was a sissy, and people made fun of him. But we loved him."

I told her that I considered his first book, *Other Voices, Other Rooms*, a sad account of childhood. But I wondered if its mostly glowing New York reviews in 1948 influenced her decision to move there. "Not really," she answered. "I moved there because I wanted to live in an exciting big city and become a writer." Perhaps so. But the coincidence of Truman's well-received novel the year before she moved made Dartie and me wonder if she spoke from the bitterness of later years rather than his literary accomplishments at the time. Nephew Ed Conner agreed with Nelle, arguing that she always considered her literary gifts equal to his.

When I discussed the brooding loneliness of *Other Voices*, she responded: "Who wouldn't be lonely as a child if you were passed back and forth from one adult to another?" That response triggered Dartie's hypothesis she had long waited to test on Nelle: "It was as if you and Sook offered Truman unconditional love and genuine concern for his welfare and happiness." "Of course," she virtually shouted. "We thought his celebrity to be a hollow substitute for the maternal love and family stability he so desperately sought."

Perhaps by way of compensation, the older Truman cultivated a circle of female high-society friends. He referred to them as his "swans." Their lunchtime conversations in the city's finest restaurants and participation in his 1966 Black and White Ball at the Plaza Hotel became iconic footnotes in New York City history. On the forty-fifth anniversary of the masquerade ball, and long after Truman's death, I asked if she had attended. She replied incredulously: "You know better than that, Wayne! I did not attend that thing!" She elaborated that Truman had invited every prominent person he could think of, including President Lyndon Baines Johnson and Lady Bird. He dangled invitations as if he were scalping tickets to the Super Bowl. It indicates how little Nelle cared to be at the center of history that she ridiculed an event at which guest-of-honor Katharine Graham—publisher of the *Washington Post*—extended her journalistic influence among politicians, socialites, and intellectuals, who later supported the *Post*'s revelations about Watergate.

NELLE ALSO DESPISED TRUMAN'S narcissism, a character flaw that finally and abruptly cut him off from his swans. The downfall came when he published a scandalous series of articles in *Esquire* magazine in the mid 1970s recounting the swans' intimate revelations about their husbands' infidelities, bizarre eroticism, or anything else prurient enough to sell (the articles were posthumously published as an unfinished novel, *Answered Prayers*).

During an afternoon not long before Nelle died, I asked if Truman had lost his swans' friendships when he betrayed their confidences. "Most of them," she said sadly. "But he grieved most about losing the friendship of Babe Paley." Barbara Cushing Paley was considered one of the world's most beautiful and stylish women. Born into wealth, she gained even more through marriage to the founder of the CBS radio and television network. She had shared details of her troubled marriage and her husband's affair with the wife of a New York governor. Other than the estranged wife of late-night television star Johnny Carson—who had his own stable of mistresses, according to Nelle—Truman had few friends left when he died in 1984 at Joanne Carson's California home.

THE 1940S AND 1950S furnished no hint of the disintegration of Nelle's and Truman's friendship. One day in 1959, Truman invited her to join him on a trip that would change both their lives. Wheat farmer Herb Clutter, his wife, and two children had been brutally murdered in their farmhouse outside Garden City, Kansas. In the crease between finishing *To Kill a Mockingbird* and its publication, she welcomed the diversion. She told us that crimes had always fascinated her and that she also understood the small town and its people. But, as one biographer wrote, Truman in Garden City was like someone coming there from the moon.

When Nelle and Truman arrived by train, they discovered a town much like Monroeville except the citizens were conservative Republicans instead of conservative Democrats. And unlike Monroeville, there were practically no African Americans. Garden City was small and intimate, a place where people knew their neighbors and helped them when they needed it. Many of the 11,811 residents (Monroeville's population then was 3,632) were devout Methodists, believed in traditional values, and attended one of the town's twenty-two churches. Prohibition was long over, but given the paucity of bars, Truman thought the news had not yet reached Garden City. "No theaters, no art galleries, no bookstores," Truman mused to Nelle one night during their usual stroll. "What do they do for entertainment?" A few minutes later as they walked in silence, Nelle noticed a condom in a drain as they crossed the street, nudged Truman, pointed to the condom, and replied, "Now we know what they do at night in Garden City!"

Alvin Dewey supervised the local office of the Kansas Bureau of Investigation. Normally he might not have welcomed friendship with a flamboyant homosexual such as Capote. But his wife, Marie, was like Truman a native of New Orleans, a fan of fiction, and perhaps a bit bored with life in Garden City. She liked Truman immediately. The Deweys' then nine-year-old son Paul remembered that his mother's distinctive New Orleans accent reemerged. And Nelle was so attentive to Paul's cat, Pete, and her ritual tickling game with him, that he promised to marry her when he grew up. They became such close friends that Nelle kept up a fifty-year correspondence with Alvin, Marie, and Paul. She and Truman came by train to Garden City in 1959, 1960, and 1962, met the Deweys in Colorado once, and the Deweys traveled to New York City to be with Nelle at Truman's memorial service. Nelle also kept in touch with Dodie Hope, a columnist for the local newspaper as well as the widow of the judge who presided at the trial of the Clutters' killers.

While Truman cultivated Alvin for tidbits of information about the murders, Nelle strolled neighborhoods in her nicest dresses interviewing friends and acquaintances of the Clutters. She never took notes during the interviews, but would afterwards fill a notebook with the conversations. The townspeople, most of whom would not have warmed to Truman, liked the slow-talking, friendly, small-town Alabama Methodist woman.

One afternoon when I mentioned that the Truman Capote papers at the New York Public Library contained her notebook, she seemed surprised. She told us that she thought Truman had destroyed her notes. Perhaps that is what he told her. It was partly her notes, I believed, that allowed Truman to humanize the Clutter family in his stunning 1966 best-seller, *In Cold Blood*. Although he dedicated the book to Nelle and the writing was unmistakably Capote's, I doubted whether its contextual richness would have been possible without her notes and their long conversations about the town and its people. Nevertheless, she never expressed jealousy or claimed credit for the book when I afforded her the opportunity to do so.

When the subject surfaced again, I asked her preference among all his books. She immediately answered, "*In Cold Blood.*" I replied that though I preferred his early lyrical novels, *In Cold Blood* did introduce a new genre of literature, "creative nonfiction." She let me know in a hurry that I had moved out of historical analysis into literary criticism with a sharp rebuke: "That book did NOT introduce a new form of literature!"

Although she never responded publicly to the rumors that Truman claimed to have written *Mockingbird*, she told us that in private conversations with a small group in New York City he had done so when inflating his own importance. And on a December afternoon in 2007 she told us that Truman tended to "claim credit for anything and everything." Fortunately for history and her reputation, he told a Monroeville relative in a 1959 letter that Nelle had shown him part of her manuscript: "I liked it very much. She has real talent." That letter pretty much resolves the debate over authorship of *Mockingbird*.

Nelle later proved to be a competent movie critic when *Capote* and *Infamous* were released in 2005 and 2006, respectively, adapting his/her/their story to cinema. Both filmmakers sent Nelle advance videos of the movies, which she watched at her nephew's home in Monroeville. She complained to us that both were incorrect in numerous details. She mentioned a scene in Kansas murderer Perry Smith's prison cell where Truman tried to seduce him. Actually, neither she nor Truman were ever allowed in the murderers' cells. Ironically, Nelle, the legendarily sloppy dresser, complained that Sandra Bullock, who brilliantly played her character in *Infamous*, wore bobby socks with pumps. Nelle admitted that she might not be stylish, but she did know better than that: "Bullock has an idiot for a costume designer. It never occurred to me to wear socks with pumps, and Truman looks ready for a drag ball. Had we arrived in Kansas thus attired, people would have gone inside and kept the doors locked!" Despite many incorrect details, she demanded only one alteration: "Change the socks!" Such was her clout that the socks were changed in the final cut of the movie.

As I was driving home in 2014, I heard an interview on NPR with the producer of *Capote*. After praising Philip Seymour Hoffman's brilliant performance in the lead role, which won him an Academy Award, he said that he treasured even more Harper Lee's vintage hand-written note to him gently criticizing inaccurate details but adding that fiction writers, artists, and filmmakers had to fuse real events with their imagination in order to create a sense of alternate reality. Then he quoted Nelle: "You told the truth about Truman!"

Not long before Nelle's death, I asked if the late 1960s rupture in their friendship had resulted from Truman's jealousy of her Pulitzer Prize and his failure to win any of America's most prestigious literary prizes. Or was she, like Truman's long-time partner Jack Dunphy, who also broke with him during that period, simply unwilling to watch while Capote destroyed himself with promiscuity, drugs, and alcohol. I knew this was an intensely personal question and that she had her own problems with alcohol during those years. She deftly avoided my question by redefining it: "I did not push him away. He pushed me away."

In our sixty-four afternoons during a decade of visits, that was the most poignant moment. Dartie recorded one of the longest pauses in our conversations as the three of us struggled for words. Many years later during an oral history, one of her closest friends told me perceptively: "Nelle's loyalty was absolute; but when it was gone, IT WAS GONE!"

After I finished a year reading virtually everything Truman Capote wrote in preparation for an essay I was writing about him, I asked Nelle if the melancholia so persistent in his early prose resulted from his "sad childhood." "What sad childhood?" she snapped. "He was the most spoiled child I ever knew. He was the only child in Monroeville to have a charge account at the pharmacy!" On the way home that afternoon, Dartie and I fretted about how charge accounts sometimes became surrogates for the attention and love vulnerable children desperately need.

On a subsequent visit, I launched our final conversation about Truman's place in American literature. She cut me short and did not invite further questions: "I did not like him!" We were shocked. No doubt she conflated their childhood friendship with the later unraveling. Neither of us knew what to say, so Dartie recorded yet another awful silence.

I know it is a contradiction of what Nelle told us that afternoon, but Dartie and I preferred a different ending to this story of friendship betrayed and lost. As some literary critics have speculated, we believe a passage in *Mockingbird* about Scout's fictional friend Dill is really about Truman: "Beautiful things floated in his dreamy head." He was a boy who "preferred his own twilight world, a world where babies slept, waiting to be gathered like morning lilies."

UPON ARRIVAL IN THE Big Apple, Nelle rented a one-bedroom cold water flat in an aged red brick building whose ripped blue awning flapped in the wind. From her description, it must have been an embarrassment to residents of more elegant residences on Manhattan's Upper East Side. She bragged that post-war rent control made the fifteen-dollar-a-month apartment one of the city's great bargains due to its run-down condition. When she finally earned enough, she enjoyed walking to nearby Manelli's Italian restaurant on 82nd Street.

Dartie asked if she cooked in the tiny kitchen. Nelle replied in disbelief as if Dartie were questioning her culinary skill: "Of course I cooked! It was cook or starve." Embarrassed by Nelle's misinterpretation of her question, Dartie asked what she cooked. Nelle was silent for a moment, then laughed: "Spaghetti!" I followed up with my own question since obviously even Italians eat something other than pasta: "Did you have a favorite restaurant?" "Yes," she laughed, "a bar on 79th Street."

Initially, her tight budget obviously restricted her food options and transportation. She walked, took a bus, or the subway wherever she went, never a taxi. The anonymity that many Southern expatriates found devastating, she found exhilarating. As she wrote in *Watchman*: "In New York you are your own person. You may reach out and embrace all of Manhattan in sweet aloneness, or you can go to hell if you want to."

In time, fame and fortune provided fancier cuisine at the legendary Plaza Hotel and the Russian Tea Room and a broader range of entertainment conforming to her whims and lifelong interest in sports, chief among them being the New York Mets baseball team.

Shea Stadium in Queens was a short subway ride away. Although the Mets' 1962 initial season was the worst in modern baseball history, the acquisition of pitcher Tom Seaver—who would become a three-time recipient of the Cy Young Award, winner of 311 games, and a Hall of Famer—transformed the team from the butt of jokes into a title contender. In 1969 Seaver and the "Miracle Mets" beat the Baltimore Orioles to win the World Series. For Nelle, summer afternoons and evenings at Shea, eating hot dogs, watching Seaver pitch and the Mets win, didn't quite match winning the Pulitzer Prize, but it would do until she finished her next novel.

ANOTHER NOVEL, HOWEVER, REQUIRED the confidence to move on and the solitary, disciplined life of a writer. She may not have had either at the time. Disengaging from her routine for part of the summer on Fire Island seemed a promising enforced solitude. Unfortunately, as she told us one afternoon decades later, she had loved to fish while growing up in Monroe County, and on Fire Island she met a retired boat captain who spent his time devoted to that recreation. Her best intentions dissipated in a bait can and the surf. Being a devoted creek-bank fisherman myself, I joked that if she had not been so devoted to fishing, she might have been a more productive writer. She shot back: "So would you!" In trading insults, she was not to be trifled with.

Such diversions to writing became common after publication of *To Kill a Mockingbird*. Teenager Cammie Plummer, daughter of the booksellers who helped organize Harper Lee's speaking event in Mobile, Alabama, came north in 1963 on her way to join the freshmen class at Wellesley College. Nelle remembered the royal treatment the Plummers had bestowed on her in Mobile and reciprocated with a week for Cammie in the Roosevelt Hotel. The two Alabamians had a good time, laughing together at the racy new film, *Tom Jones*, eating at Nelle's favorite restaurants, shopping at a nearby bookstore. Cammie told me one of her favorite Harper Lee stories, one that cast light on the life of an obscure and private person suddenly in the spotlight. After Nelle wrote a check to pay for books, the clerk carefully scrutinized the check, especially the signature. *Mockingbird* had been published only three years earlier, and the clerk vaguely remembered the author's name: "Isn't there a book, something about killing a mockingbird?" "Yes," Nelle replied. "My sister wrote that!"

Another treat that week was watching President John F.

Kennedy's motorcade to the United Nations where he would be speaking about the Cuban missile crisis. They stood for a long time amidst a huge crowd packing the sidewalks near the U.N. headquarters. Growing concerned about Nelle, Cammie finally said that they could leave if she was tired. Nelle insisted they remain: "I think you ought to see the president. It may be your only chance to see a president in person."

So far as we knew, Nelle never neglected friends or even acquaintances from Alabama who were visiting New York. Years later, writer Wayne Greenhaw, a lifelong friend from her literary circle at the University of Alabama, won the Harper Lee Award presented annually by the Alabama Writers' Symposium. After he was presented the award in Monroeville, he stopped by her assisted living facility to talk with her. We happened to be there, so he told us this story.

Greenhaw had business with his publisher in New York City and arranged to have lunch with Nelle at the Russian Tea Room. She arrived early, but his flight was delayed by stormy weather. In desperation, he asked to use the plane's phone to call her. She told him not to worry. She had brought a book of Eudora Welty's short stories to read while she waited. When he finally arrived an hour late, embarrassed, she brushed aside his apology, telling him, "Eudora Welty entertained me splendidly."

HER BIRTHDAY IN 2012 coincided as it often did with the Alabama Writers' Symposium. That year, her friend, novelist Fannie Flagg, won the prize named in Harper Lee's honor. Flagg was the author of one of Dartie's favorite novels, *Fried Green Tomatoes at the Whistle Stop Cafe*, later made into one of our favorite movies.

She and Nelle became friends after Flagg, as she had a decade earlier, fled Alabama for the "Big Apple."

George Landegger—Connecticut billionaire and CEO of Parsons and Whittemore, whose two paper mills in Monroe County had become the largest local employer—was also the generous underwriter of the annual symposium. The day Flagg was to get the prize, he drove to Nelle's assisted living facility. She greeted him by asking where he was going so dressed up. He told her that he had come for her, because Fannie Flagg was about to receive the award named in her honor. As far as we knew, she had never attended the symposium even in perfect health, and since her stroke she had attended no public events. But Landegger was unrelenting, and Flagg was a friend. So off she went in her wheelchair to the glitzy event, dressed in her typical frumpy slacks, a T-shirt, without makeup or even combing her hair. The audience of several hundred writers, their fans, and teachers of literature could not have been more astounded if the President of the United States had walked into the room.

Flagg was so overwhelmed that she cast aside her prepared speech and told this story. While a young cohost of a Birmingham television show, earning fifty dollars a week, she was denied a raise by her male station manager, who said she would probably marry and leave anyway. Flagg was furious, quit her job, and moved to New York City with dreams of writing a novel. The day she received a rejection letter, she went for a walk to assuage her disappointment and to ease the pain in her back. A man who needed either an attitude adjustment or perhaps a mental hospital crossed a busy street and told her she was really ugly. The combination of literary rejection, throbbing back pain, and gratuitous insult was more than she could bear, so she broke into tears. Proceeding on to her chiropractor's office, she was greeted by a young male receptionist who recognized a familiar Southern accent. He asked where she was from. "Birmingham," she answered. He was from Monroeville, and recognizing her pain and unhappiness, invited her to join him that evening to attend a reading and lecture by Eudora Welty. She agreed, and following the lecture, he introduced her to his Monroeville friend, Harper Lee, who had also attended. After Flagg had described her terrible day, an empathetic Nelle told her: "Don't ever give up. Just keep on trying!"

By the time Flagg delivered the punch line, there were not many dry eyes in the auditorium. Except Nelle's, because she had heard nothing Flagg said. We stopped by her room that afternoon and mentioned the excitement at the "Harper Lee sighting." But having heard nothing, she remembered nothing. It was her birthday, however, and the room was filled with a huge floral arrangement of tulips and a card sent by Oprah Winfrey. I measured the mountain of flowers—four feet long and two feet high, so large that after the delivery driver left, the staff moved the display to the commons area where all could enjoy the burst of color and fragrance. The floral gift was an annual Winfrey tradition after Harper Lee wrote an essay for the Christmas edition of *O, The Oprah Magazine*.

WHEN WE RETURNED HOME and I opened our accumulated mail, I found a package of nominees for election to the Alabama Academy of Honor. The Academy consists of one hundred living Alabamians who have made major contributions to the state. Members— Harper Lee was inducted in 2007—can nominate candidates to fill vacancies, with the inductees chosen by a vote of the current members. Among the nominees in 2012 was Alice Lee, nominated by her little sister, Nelle. We could not ignore the irony of Nelle's detailed listing of Alice's qualifications for membership: America's oldest practicing female attorney; a sterling legal career in tax law; first woman elected to lead the Alabama-West Florida Conference of the Methodist Church; many civic awards and club presidencies; unofficial historian of Southwest Alabama.

Nelle's earlier election to the Academy resulted from authorship of a single book. Her accomplishment was like a meteor's flight, dazzling the world as it broke through the sky above New York City. Alice's honor was more that of the tortoise, never moving fast or straying far from home, but steady and determined in its attention to its parochial environment, careful and measured in its progress so as not to endanger its habitat.

Chapter 7

Mockingbird: The Book

ON MORE THAN ONE AFTERNOON WHEN WE TOLD NELLE STORIES about her fame, she swept aside the flattery by responding, "All I did was write a book." Dartie just as routinely corrected her: "No, Nelle! You wrote a book for the ages." So often did she chant the mantra that we concluded it was her way of deflecting attention or even adulation. As Ed Conner, her professor of literature nephew, put it, "She knew that all Boris Pasternak, Margaret Mitchell, Emily Bronte, and Ralph Ellison did was 'write a book.'"

To Kill a Mockingbird indeed was a story for the ages. During the eighty years from 1895 to 1975, it was the third best-selling novel in America and seventh best among all books. Fans purchased two and a half million copies the first year. It remained on the *New York Times* best-seller list for eighty-eight weeks. Sales then declined to *only* one million copies a year for decades, boosted by required-reading lists in American, Irish, Australian, New Zealand, and British schools and in many other parts of the world. Perhaps no book other than the Bible has been so universally read and studied in the past century. In 1999, Amazon users rated it the third-best book written in the twentieth century, and American librarians voted it the best novel of the century. A 1989 survey of novels required in American Catholic, public, and private schools ranked *Mockingbird* respectively fourth, fourth, and fifth. Lee was the only living author with a book in the top ten. When the Library of Congress polled its patrons about books that "had made a difference in their lives," the novel ranked second only to the Bible. In the March 2007 annual World Book Day poll in the United Kingdom, respondents listed novels by Jane Austen, J. R. R. Tolkien, Charlotte Bronte, and J. K. Rowling in the first four places, *Mockingbird* fifth, and the Bible sixth. Lee herself was disturbed by the low ranking of the King James Bible.

While attempting to rejuvenate reading among British teenagers in 2014, a survey reported that *Mockingbird* was their third favorite book. Australians voted it their favorite American novel. In 2003, Publishing Triangle—an association of gay, lesbian, transgender, and bisexual publishers—listed *Mockingbird* as one of the best gay novels because so many lesbians identified with Scout's bravery, independence, and outsider status.

Amazingly, as the novel approached three-quarters of a century of life amid increasing controversy, it achieved its greatest triumph since the Pulitzer Prize in 1960. On May 22, 2018, the Public Broadcasting Service (PBS) launched a six-month, eight-part series to determine the nation's favorite novel and author. The criteria stipulated that nominated books should open readers' minds, describe national diversity, and explore the human experience.

Dartie and I voted once a day as allowed by the rules, then watched the final ranking that October. The host of the series heightened the drama by beginning at Number 10 and counting down. As obvious contenders such as Jane Austen, Mark Twain, William Faulkner, and Ernest Hemingway were eliminated, we already knew America's favorite novel and author and began our celebration. However, we were stunned to learn that *Mockingbird* had ranked first every day of the marathon contest, swamping all contenders. We also contemplated what it would have been like to share that evening with Nelle in The Meadows, her assisted living home, had she not died nineteen months earlier. Our mourning turned to laughing when we simultaneously quoted her dismissive response to our high fives and hugs at other awards or moments of fame: "All I did was write a book!"

Seldom in the history of American literature has a novel so enthralled, educated, and humanized ordinary readers while being so casually dismissed by literary critics and scholars. But from a wider view, a breach between elite and folk culture has always existed, amid a less obvious gap between popular novels such as *To Kill a Mockingbird* and innovative fiction such as James Joyce's *Ulysses*.

As generations passed since 1960, contemporary events in American history as well as familiar divisions between elite and non-elite Americans have shaped attitudes about *Mockingbird*. Historical debates also have played a role. Shifting attitudes about race, arguments over the efficacy of gradualism compared to revolutionary and violent change, philosophical differences about how to measure integrity, courage, and enlightenment—are such virtues contingent on time and place or measured by some universal standard of what is always required of honorable men and women?—tend to be both generational and fierce: "My way or the highway!"

Caught in the maelstrom of such post-1960 debates, Lee's "racial enlightenment" by 1960 standards seemed increasingly arcane and reactionary by 2021 benchmarks. When the Modern Library recruited a dozen literary scholars to determine the "one hundred best novels in the twentieth century" so the rest of us would not waste our time on frivolous reading, *To Kill a Mockingbird* did not make the list despite its continuing global popularity.

I CONFESS MY PERSONAL bias as a participant in this intellectual debate. I spent nearly my entire sixty-year academic career studying history from the bottom up instead of from the top down. My prism of the past was shaped by family and place like nearly everyone else's. My people were working class: sharecroppers, tenant farmers, carpenters, electricians, workers in steel mills and automobile tire plants, salesmen. They did not read James Joyce or William Faulkner. I wrote about hard-working, poor but proud blacks and whites, their religion, families, pastimes, athletic accomplishments, and alternative culture. I came of age in the 1960s, earned my PhD amid unprecedented challenges to every American norm, and challenged traditional accounts and omissions within the narrative of the American past. By my standard, Lee's novel was a radical challenge to Southern literary tradition—the story of a decent, conservative, white, iconic figure in a conflicted small Southern town who defied its racial pathology. His allies were a mixture of "his own people" (sheriff, judge, some fellow church members), but also Dixie's forgotten people "from 'Old Sarum'" such as Walter Cunningham, the last hold-out on the Maycomb County jury that convicted Tom Robinson. My preferred books were about ordinary people: Zora Neale Hurston's *Their Eyes Were Watching God* and James Agee and Walker Evans's *Let Us Now Praise Famous Men*.

Literary critics and presentist historians sometimes create their own alternative historical reality. How different would the fate of Tom Robinson have been in the 1930s Deep South if the southern headquarters of the American Communist Party in Birmingham had launched a national campaign to save Tom Robinson? Absent twenty-twenty hindsight, did the legal strategy chosen at that time by Atticus Finch in the most racist swath of America—the Deep South's Black Belt—or the courageous and career-ending ruling of Judge Horton in the more "liberal" Tennessee Valley offer the best hope of acquittal of a black man accused of raping a white woman when the verdict would be determined by an all-white, all-male jury?

At the end of the two trials, one fictional, the other actual, Atticus Finch (modeled on A. C. Lee) remained a respected arbiter of justice and retained influence in Maycomb (Monroeville). At the end of the Scottsboro case, Judge Horton was defeated for reelection, and his successor took no such risks. So far as influencing future public policy, Horton may as well have relocated to China.

As a historian of Alabama, what I could not understand was the assumption that a small-town newspaper publisher and attorney during the Great Depression could have been either a twentieth-century prophet like Jeremiah or a civil rights icon like John Lewis. Such a person in such a time would have sailed against the current of his time. It was my historical judgment that he would have been either a martyr or an exile, incapable either way of being an agent of gradual change. At best he would have been ignored. Numerous painful memoirs, autobiographies, and biographies describe the fate of Southern prophetic voices between 1930 and 1970. And while martyrdom plays its role in the vast human odyssey, so does gradualism, which is the historical saga of how society changes by erosion from inside a culture rather than assault from outside. Both are useful strategies at alternative stages of historical transition.

Of no less importance is how Harper Lee structured her narrative. *Mockingbird*'s fictional father-figure was not temperamentally or ideologically inclined toward social upheaval. Based on my research, interviews, and correspondence with people of differing genders, ages, temperaments, political, economic, ideological, and racial views, I came to "know" Atticus Finch/Coley Lee as well as a historian can "know" a person he never met. By all estimates A. C. Lee was a decent, honorable, nonviolent man, a good and kindly neighbor, a faithful caregiver to his afflicted wife, a man who treated African Americans with respect despite his belief in their inferiority. He was a segregationist and by modern conceptions a racist. He was conservative in matters of gender, finance, race, and even Methodism. He even dressed conservatively in suits and vests with a watch fob. He worked hard to provide for his large family of a wife and four children, even the daughter who dropped out of law school and the church, abandoned Alabama for New York City, and perhaps profanely confronted him about his own racial prejudice.

To REPEAT THE CRITERIA of the Great American Read, a literary classic opens readers' minds, appreciates American diversity, and shares the human experience of tragedy and triumph. It seemed to Dartie and me that readers devoted to those criteria had no need to consult literary critics or historians to determine their favorite novel.

These were our issues. Not once in a decade of conversation with her did Nelle engage about the fame her novel had conferred on her. When we told her story after story about some new ranking, she generally changed the subject unless it had a back story. Only when it involved a contemporary, personal, human narrative did she take notice. Only once did she share a fan letter, and that from a working-class British man.

Her favorite discussions about her novel concerned translation of its title. The mockingbird is native to North America, with a range from northern Mexico to Canada, so the bird's name conveys no meaning to most people speaking the more than forty other languages into which the novel has been translated.

Because I lectured about *Mockingbird* in many countries on three continents, I always returned with lots of stories to tell Nelle. In Western Europe, "mockingbird" is usually translated as "nightingale." A Chinese student told me the title in his language was *A City Named Maycomb*. After my lecture to a class of South Korean women who had read the novel as teenagers, they told me that "mockingbird" was translated as "parrot." In Hungary, the literal Magyar translation is particularly puzzling unless you have tangled, as I have, with an angry mockingbird defending its nest: *No Quarreling with a Mockingbird!*

Following my lecture at the University of Georgia, art historian Asen Kirin told me a story that most enthralled Nelle. He grew up in a small Bulgarian town under communism. Local officials announced one day that residents would be provided a new American movie which they subsequently referred to as "To Kill a Jokester." After watching the film, officials lectured the audience about the inadequacies, racism, and hypocrisy of American democracy despite its pretensions of justice for all. Kirin and his family, along with many other townspeople, interpreted the film differently. They compared the aspirations for fairness and justice depicted by Atticus, Dill, Jem, Scout, Miss Maudie, the judge, sheriff, and others to the injustice of the prosecutor and jurors. The "joke" was on totalitarian Bulgarian officials who forced them to watch a movie that subverted support for their own regime.

Divergent titles revealed different meanings that translators, like readers, derived from the book concerning honor, courage, and the moral obligation to defy community traditions and institutions on behalf of justice.

Nelle had her own stories about translations, the funniest from the Netherlands. They queried forty-seven words and phrases that had no exact Dutch equivalent including "spite fences," "Haints," "homemade divinity," "grit paper," and "chunked at her."

After our next visit, I had more evidence of both the novel's metaphorical "songs" and the occasional bizarre meaning people attributed to them. A column by Pulitzer Prize-winning Alabama journalist John Archibald praised prophetic Southern critics of the region's shortcomings as the real "mockingbirds." He included Harper Lee as foremost among these "beautiful people." She seemed amazed and delighted by this designation.

To balance her pleasure at this praise, we gave her a clipping from the *Wall Street Journal* describing a Florida attorney's reference to *Mockingbird* when defending the killer of a black teenager. She was already aware of the use and misuse of her novel in legal proceedings, so this was no surprise. Nonetheless, it was a painful disappointment.

I continued the afternoon's conversation by brief summaries of reactions from different audiences where I had lectured recently. One of my former Auburn students had invited me to speak to thirty-five Illinois social studies teachers. I began, as I often do, by asking how many had read the novel. Only one had not. That same week I lectured to six hundred Auburn University honors students, only twelve of whom had not read it.

Of the three anecdotes I shared with her that day, her favorite involved ninety passengers on the iconic *Delta Queen*, a 1920s paddlewheel steamboat. They were older, affluent, well-educated Americans, Canadians, and Brits. To provoke a conversation, I mentioned the recent *Modern Library* ranking of the hundred best novels in English published during the twentieth century, which had omitted *Mockingbird*. First place belonged to *Ulysses* by James Joyce. I asked if anyone had read *Ulysses*. One woman raised her hand. Naughty as it was of me, I asked if she had completed the novel or stopped before the end. She blushed and stammered sufficiently for all of us to know the answer before she confessed. I then explained that some novels engross people but to other people are just gross. Her answer actually was the key to my lecture because I then asked, "How many of you have read ALL of *Mockingbird*?" Either some passengers lied or *all* had read the entire novel. Just in case, I had prepared two lectures, one if everyone had read *Mockingbird*, a different lecture if I had to summarize the characters and plot.

Nelle and her sisters had traveled down the Mississippi River on the *Delta Queen*, and she was astounded at my audacity when I was being paid to entertain rather than to embarrass passengers. I asked her why I should spend time summarizing the plot of a book that everyone had already read?

DURING HALF A CENTURY lecturing about Harper Lee and her second novel in countries as disparate as China and Ireland, I had concluded that the only book shared in common by more inhabitants of the globe was the Bible, which did not necessarily please her given her high regard for the King James translation of that book. I explained that when I preached about Jesus, I quoted the Bible. But when I lectured about justice in Alabama or America, or about judging other people, I quoted Harper Lee because the audiences were more familiar with her work than God's teachings on the subject.

Nelle's favorite "Flynt *Mockingbird*" story began with a March 2013 email from the producer of "Books and Arts Daily" on Radio National, Australia's public radio network. The host was devoting a month to American literature and had polled listeners about their favorite among forty authors and novels. The audience had chosen Harper Lee and *Mockingbird*. The host had selected a panel consisting of Mary Murphy, director of the splendid "American Masters" PBS documentary about Lee and her novel; several perceptive Australian literary critics; a fourteen-year-old student who was currently reading the novel; and me for the live discussion.

My homework for the program began with a visit to my Australian neighbors in Auburn, Chris and Sue Rodger. I asked if they had read the novel while growing up in Sydney. They explained that when the novel was assigned in their early high school years, it seemed to be a uniquely American story about race in the South. Nonetheless, they both loved the characterizations of Jem, Dill, and Scout, as well as the marvelous storytelling. Sue particularly identified with Scout, whom she described as defiant, daring, courageous, independent, and risk-taking. At the all-girls school Sue attended, her girlfriends giggled at the discussion of sex but were more deeply affected by the obvious injustice. Chris relished brief discussions of football and the children's misjudgment of their father's "manliness."

Following my interview with the Rodgers, I began reading about Sydney. It was by then a quite different place than the one they remembered. It had grown to 4.6 million people, one-third born abroad. In the Parramatta suburb, half the residents were born outside Australia, most in Asia or the Middle East. As in many of the world's great migrant urban centers, early arrivers considered newer ones "different" and less able to assimilate. Ethnic tensions had increased as newcomers arrived and working-class residents descended from British and Irish families were pushed out or voluntarily moved. The aborigine identity movement had also reached urban areas from the Outback.

While the radio program was live, Australian listeners flooded the airways with stories for two hours, mostly expressing adoration for the novel and its elusive author. I punctured Nelle's rapt attention and ego by reading my notes about one Aussie grouch who declared her novel to be "simplistic, parochial, and juvenile." That denunciation inspired another caller named Michael. Michael described himself as having been a miserable child who was bullied by other students. So awful was the abuse that he was contemplating suicide when his teacher assigned *Mockingbird*. As he began to read, he was enthralled by the novel, especially by "Boo" Radley. Radley was like him: isolated, stereotyped, different, misunderstood. Michael decided to emulate Boo, who was confident of his own worth even if he was a largely unknown hero by the end of the book. After completing school, he became a successful businessman, naming his company after Atticus Finch in honor of the novel's hero.

Nelle was mesmerized. Dartie told me on the way home that when I finished the story, Nelle seemed lost in her own solitude before emerging with her mantra for deflecting praise: "All I did was write a book!" But Dartie noted that this time Nelle's tone of voice had changed from jocular and dismissive to reflective.

On our next visit, I described how our son Sean had served as a teaching assistant in Krems, Austria. Knowing his Alabama origins, the teacher invited him to speak about the novel. To help the students connect to distant culture and place, he showed them a photo of a parade in Austria during the same period as *Mockingbird*, when their own great-grandparents welcomed Hitler. The world of that photo might seem as alien to them as *Mockingbird* seemed to him, he explained, but shaped their present world in much the same way that racism shaped and haunted the modern American South.

Nelle listened intently to my account, then countered with her own. She once escorted an Austrian visitor on a walking tour of New York City. When they came to a square celebrating a number of distinguished New Yorkers such as the Rockefeller family, her visitor dismissively summarized them in two words: "All Jews!" Nelle pointed out that actually the Rockefellers were Baptists, and none of the other persons celebrated on the square were Jews. She hoped that Sean's story meant that younger Austrians were becoming better informed and less anti-Semitic.

One cold afternoon in 2015, we carried her an issue of the

newspaper *USA Today* which included a weekly list of best-selling books. *Mockingbird* ranked forty-ninth in its fifty-fifth year of publication. Not many such events impressed her. This one did, ironically not for the ranking but for the book's longevity. She muttered over and over as if she had forgotten the publication date: "fifty-fifth year . . . fifty-fifth year." I placed the list on her magnifier, joking that I had highlighted it in Auburn University's colors of orange and blue so she would remember the source of this good news. That set her to laughing, ending her preoccupation with aging book and author.

When we returned two months later for Nelle's eighty-eighth birthday, we had yet another *Mockingbird* anecdote to add to her expanding collection. We had watched a segment of the PBS series "Antiques Roadshow" that featured a woman from Tuscaloosa, Alabama. She had brought her first edition of *To Kill a Mockingbird* for evaluation. The initial printing of five thousand copies had sold out immediately on the way to millions sold during the first year of publication. I had seen one pristine copy signed by both Harper Lee and Truman Capote advertised in the *New York Times* for $74,000. The "Roadshow" guest was Tay Hohoff's granddaughter. She and her mother lived in Tuscaloosa at the time of Hohoff's visit and arranged a cocktail party in Nelle's honor. The woman, then a young girl of seven or eight, asked if she could attend the party. Her mother consented with one condition: If she misbehaved, she would have to leave. Like most young children at adult parties, she found the adults boring, caused trouble, and was exiled to the back steps. Not long afterwards, she heard the door open and someone sat down beside her. When she looked up, Harper Lee was sitting next to her. They talked until the party was nearly over. That evening Nelle autographed the first edition to her editor and friend: "Tay, for your kindness editing the book." Although the copy was worn and the dust jacket frayed, the "Roadshow's" book specialist estimated its worth at $12,000 to $15,000. I told Nelle that given the provenance, I thought the estimate too low. She quipped, "No book is worth that except a first edition of the King James Bible!" "Right, Nelle," I laughed, "and for many of your worldwide fans, it IS the King James Bible of fiction!"

ON AUGUST 8, 2015, after publication of *Go Set a Watchman*, I took Nelle another issue of *USA Today* listing *Watchman* second in sales nationwide and *Mockingbird* up to eighth place. We had just returned from a visit with our children in Seattle so the story of the day involved my trip to my favorite bookstore, Third Place Books, within walking distance of their house. Former President Jimmy Carter had signed his new book there the previous day, so it ranked first in sales on the daily poster the store displayed. Newly published *Watchman* came in a close second and earned an equally large advertising poster next to one for *Mockingbird*. We brought her photographs of both displays.

Tonya Gold, a *London Times* writer who covered the *Watchman* story and had interviewed me, sent a first British edition purchased at a bookshop in Piccadilly that claims to be the original royal bookstore and the oldest in London, dating from 1797. We spent the remainder of that afternoon with Nelle discussing our favorite British antiquarian bookstores.

Not all visits went so well. After I stepped out of the room to talk with a nurse on our next visit, Dartie told me on the way home that she tried to lift the gloom by telling Nelle she was famous wherever we went in the world. She muttered, "No one knows me." What's more, she didn't want others to know her, only to know about her book.

Many themes in *Mockingbird*—racism and racial injustice; attempts by some Southern whites to act justly; the humanization of black and white fictional characters by moving beyond stereotypes; the limitations of religion to achieve justice in American society; contested community values—were not taken seriously even in 1960, nor are they perfected in America two-thirds of a century later. Incidents eerily similar to the legal lynching of Tom Robinson occurred nationwide in 2021 that called into question every shibboleth about American democracy. I can make the case that Monroeville has moved further from where it was in 1960 on the freedom road than most of America has since then, and that Alabama racism is not much different in quality or quantity from that toxic "virus" nationwide.

Although hindsight reveals flaws in the moral and ethical terrain of any book moving toward its centenary, *Mockingbird*'s impact can best be tracked by its influence on young people who typically read it in their mid-teens and by school systems that ban it.

In Richmond, Virginia, last capital of the Confederacy, the Hanover County School Board banned *Mockingbird* from classrooms and libraries as soon as it was published, deeming it "immoral." Unfortunately for the school board, its ban provoked two implacable foes, the gifted editor of the Richmond *News Leader* and Harper Lee. The editor created the Beadle Bumble Fund, a title derived from the literary imagination of Charles

Dickens as displayed in his novel *Oliver Twist*. The newspaper gave away fifty free copies of *Mockingbird* to redress "the stupidities of public officials." Nelle sent the editor a contribution to the fund together with one of her most clever satires:

> Surely it is plain to the simplest intelligence that *To Kill a Mockingbird* spells out in words of seldom more than two syllables a code of honor and conduct, Christian in its ethic, that is the heritage of all Southerners. To hear that the novel is "immoral" makes me count the days to 1984 for I have yet to come across a better example of doublethink.
>
> I feel, however, that the problem is one of illiteracy, not Marxism. Therefore, I enclose a small contribution to the Beadle Bumble Fund that I hope will be used to enroll the Hanover County School Board in any first grade of its choice.

Nelle had died before the Burbank, California, school system banned her novel in 2020 because one family complained that use of the "n-word" caused their child "anguish." I had no problem visualizing steam rising up in heaven nor the source of it.

By the time of the Burbank decision, most book banning had moved north to more "liberal" venues. James LaRue, director of the American Library Association's Office for Intellectual Freedom noted that the reason most often given for banning *Mockingbird* was the strong language and its discussion of race and sexuality that "makes people uncomfortable." He denounced the bans, arguing that the book resulted in "important decisions among students concerning racial tolerance," especially during a year in which thirty-six hate crimes were reported in American libraries, including graffiti on walls, racist epithets, anti-Semitic slurs, ripped-up copies of the Quran, and threats to Muslim girls wearing the hijab. In such times, he continued, *Mockingbird*'s message of racial justice and tolerance was as relevant as when the novel was first published. According to the American Library Association, Harper Lee's novel ranked seventh among banned books in 2017, including in Biloxi, Mississippi, and Duluth, Minnesota.

The year prior to the ban in Burbank, an Alabama high school English teacher described the outcome LaRue extolled. She had read the most dramatic portion of the courtroom scene from *Mockingbird* to her class. As it often does, this triggered an animated conversation among the teenagers. One student said: "I just can't understand why [jurors] can't accept the evidence." The teacher deflected the question to an African American boy who replied with trembling voice and gathering tears: "I never realized how hard it was to be an ordinary, decent human and be judged by only your skin. I wonder if I could have done it? Are there any more Atticuses in the world?" He then walked out of class in tears. After gathering himself, he returned and told the teacher: "Thank you for requiring us to read that. I don't think I will ever forget how I felt and Jem felt at the end of that trial."

The empathetic teacher who recorded that classroom epiphany added her own commentary: "I have been near tears the rest of the day hoping I didn't commit some terrible mistake. . . . I just hope I didn't do that sweet boy a disservice."

IF NOT FOR HARPER Lee's provocative novel and such sensitive and caring teachers, where will teenagers confront America's original sin? Where will these cross-racial conversations occur?

In workplaces? In churches? In social clubs? Not likely. What other single, universal, literary experience speaks more simply and profoundly to the deepest historical wounds in all nations and societies before the cynicism of adulthood swallows youthful innocence? It is an illusion to assume that growing up in America will spare teenagers "anguish" when they first encounter our genocide toward Native Americans, the injustice done to Japanese-Americans during the 1940s, the bombings of synagogues, the attacks on Asian Americans after presidential references to the "China virus." Blocking such discussions in high schools only transfers the burden to college history professors and religious leaders who, given the trajectory of American history, have been less than successful in their efforts.

Given such reactions to *Mockingbird* during recent decades, we understood Nelle's trepidation when the book was published in 1960. She had lived for more than a decade in New York City. Following the novel's publication, she feared she might have no other residential options. The book's conflicted initial reception made her decision to travel to Mobile, Alabama, only fifty miles from Monroeville, for one of her first public author appearances either a supreme moment of serendipity or a bold provocation deep in her own land.

Cameron McRae Plummer, who invited her to speak, had arrived in Mobile from Virginia in 1916 with his father, the new rector of All Saints Episcopal Church. The day they arrived, a major hurricane struck the city, which may have been an omen of events to follow.

Cameron spent his youth as a seaman traveling the world before settling down and marrying Mary Francis Young, who grew up in North Carolina. She had served as an Episcopal social worker and missionary in Appalachia before moving to Mobile as director of religious education at Christ Episcopal Church where she met Cameron; they married in 1944.

He and a friend opened the Haunted Book Shop in a building near the waterfront. Drawing on his seafaring years, he specialized in cheap paperbacks suitable for seamen on long, boring voyages. Mixed among the pulp fiction were some serious books of local and state history and many valuable antiquarian books. It became our favorite Mobile bookstore long before we knew the Lees or Plummers.

Slowly roaming the bookstore when attending various historical meetings, we noticed that Mary Francis seemed suspicious of us. We were sufficiently irregular customers for her to forget that we had ever been there; we were typically over-dressed because of other meetings; we came during normal work hours rather than at lunch breaks, and we meticulously explored books in rooms that meandered in every direction out of sight of Mary Francis who monitored the cash register. When there were no other customers, we noticed her trailing us with considerable concern. We understood her scrutiny. The bookstore also sold rare coins, and its location in a seedy neighborhood near the harbor made it subject to petty theft by "customers," night-time burglaries, and even one police shoot-out in which a robber was killed on the street outside the store.

The Plummers were active Episcopalians, patrons of the city library, symphony, civic music association, and art museum. Their extensive circle of friends and acquaintances included the wealthy and well-connected as well as eccentric free thinkers such as Eugene Walter, a founding contributor to *The Paris Review* and who represented the city's polyglot, iconoclastic culture.

Like all bookstore owners, the Plummers carefully scrutinized pre-publication book marketing for titles that might have local appeal. When they first read Lippincott's announcement of *To Kill a Mockingbird* by a woman from southwest Alabama, they realized immediately both the civic pride and lucrative financial opportunity to showcase a Monroeville writer in a city where so many of Nelle's neighbors shopped. The small press run of only five thousand copies of a book by a hitherto unknown writer did not immediately attract big-city American attention, so Plummer pitched the opportunity to come to Mobile to speak. He then utilized his wide circle of friends from the Rotary Club, Chamber of Commerce, the locally renowned Waterman shipping family, and others, to create a long-remembered event. The matriarch of the Waterman family offered Nelle the hospitality of the family mansion, and the Chamber of Commerce prepared a scroll to be presented in her honor.

Nelle explained her attitude about the occasion to the Plummers, whom she forever afterwards referred to as "Beloved International Brotherhood of Plummers": "As for the Waterman mansion, she expressed a preference for a cot in the back of the Haunted Book Shop." She also explained that she was spending most of her time working with a Dutch translator trying to explain idiomatic words and phrases. She was tempted to write him that before he could translate *Mockingbird* into Dutch, he needed to translate it from "Southern" into English.

The evening of her presentation revealed lots about Harper Lee in 1961: her unease in social situations; concern about

Alabama's reaction to what many would consider a radical race book; paralyzing fear and anxiety when speaking in public. Cammie Plummer, the daughter mentioned earlier, remembered that her parents took Nelle to lunch before the lecture, and she began with a martini, then a double, followed by a triple. By the time she arrived at the Mobile Public Library to speak, she seemed more "mellow" than drunk. But an auditorium full of "blue-haired" matriarchs, club women, and the city's business elite, few of whom were likely to embrace the novel's central messages, created even more anxiety.

Following the introduction, Nelle proceeded to the lectern, where she scandalized the audience by removing her low-heeled shoes—because they hurt her feet—before beginning the lecture. Two years later amid great fame, Nelle remembered that evening and the Plummers' support with such affection that it led to life-long friendships and Nelle's reciprocal hospitality for Cammie on her way to Wellesley. Nelle and Alice had also sent Cammie a high school graduation present.

Cammie later dropped out of college to marry P. D. East, a liberal labor union activist, newspaper publisher, and advocate of desegregation while living in Petal, Mississippi. An alleged $250,000 Ku Klux Klan bounty to murder East forced his relocation to the iconoclastic community of Fairhope, Alabama, where he met Cammie. Many of her friends were scandalized by the engagement to a political radical and divorced man. But when the couple spent an evening with Nelle in New York City, Nelle squeezed her hand tightly and whispered, "Good for you, baby." East once told Nelle that he "might as well play the role of a bastard" and asked if she was writing another book. She said she was writing "about a murder in north Alabama"—which became the unpublished "The Reverend," which we will get to later.

After East's death, Cammie married Bill Cowan. Following art study at local Spring Hill College, Cowan attended the renowned Art Institute of Chicago, Yale, and the Frank Lloyd Wright Institute. He became a successful Mobile artist and taught art at the University of Notre Dame until he angered an administrator by refusing to raise the grade assigned an athlete. Cowan soon concluded he had no long-term future there. Despite their friendship, Nelle sometimes offended Cowan with her off-hand criticisms of Catholicism. Although a non-practicing Catholic, Cowan had attended Mobile's Jesuit college and had taught at the most prominent American Catholic university. But after she got to know him, Nelle confided to Cammie, "You have good taste in men."

Through the years, Nelle and Bill Cowan exchanged books and letters and had long afternoon conversations. Nelle was even inspired to paint while home in Monroeville when her father was dying. She painted portraits of him and her beloved brother Ed; according to family members, the portraits were exceptionally fine for an untrained artist.

FROM THE 1960 MOBILE library debut, fame and fortune followed Harper Lee across America on a tour that must have been more agonizing than exhilarating given her desire for privacy and dislike of public speaking. By the end of year, she was awash in royalties and was already grousing, like most authors, at the share of revenue retained by publishers.

Rather than rejoice at the wealth piling up in royalties at Lippincott and from movie revenues, Nelle told a reporter in 1963 who asked how it felt to "be getting awfully rich": "You know that program at Cape Canaveral? I'm paying for it. Ninety-five percent of the earnings disappeared in taxes." If that tax rate did apply to her earnings, the reporter's observation was correct: she was indeed becoming "awfully rich."

She became even more irascible over time, complaining about answering fan mail. We knew that she sent so many hand-written letters that the descendants of fans hoarding them would not obtain the wealth they anticipated. In 1994, a former student of mine from Monroeville was dispatched by the federal judge for whom she worked with thirty-five books for Nelle to sign. She, Nelle, and their mutual friend and local college librarian, Dale Welch, spent the afternoon reminiscing and playing Alabama trivia games while waiting impatiently for Nelle to sign the books. My student explained that Nelle "gave the distinct impression that she would much rather be out doing something else."

Decades later Nelle reluctantly continued to sign stacks of books at a local store whose owner hawked them from the back of his pickup truck to tourists waiting on the courthouse lawn for the annual amateur performance of the dramatization of *To Kill a Mockingbird* to begin. Nelle explained to us that she signed so many books to counter the exploitation of people who were charged exorbitant prices for them. I tried to explain that given her worldwide fame, signing a few hundred books at Monroeville once a year would not much diminish the international market price of a signed copy of her classic novel.

When Cammie Cowan asked what to do with her pre-publication edition of *Mockingbird*, Nelle initially told Cammie to donate it to the Alabama State Archives in Montgomery. But later, perhaps after reading the market price of a signed first edition in the *Wall Street Journal*, she told Cammie to sell it: "Then you two could take a nice little cruise."

We had our own version of the novel's worth and its effect on readers. I was completing my doctorate in Southern political history at Florida State University in 1963 while Dartie taught English in middle school. Tallahassee then was the capital of a conservative Democratic state. I had already participated in my first boycott of a restaurant that refused to serve African American FSU students. On September 15, while we watched television after church, we saw reporting of the aftermath of the bombing of Birmingham's Sixteenth Street Baptist Church. At first, we watched in horror. Then in surges of weeping. Then in indescribable anger and rage. I did not have to speculate who the murderers were, although I did not know their names. I had seen their hatred all my life in multiple faces with different names. Dartie was more shielded by her Baptist preacher-father whose sympathies were altogether with the black Baptist ministers he taught at Courtland Academy in the Tennessee Valley.

Following one of the worst days in our lives, we vowed never to live again in Alabama. For months we kept that vow. Then Dartie told me about a novel she was reading. So far as I can recall, I had read no fiction since undergraduate school. In the gap between completion of my dissertation and a post-doctoral program in East Asian history, I opened the novel Dartie recommended so highly and could not put it down. No other book, not even the Bible, had so thoroughly enthralled or deeply moved me.

When I finished reading *To Kill a Mockingbird*, Dartie and I talked about all the ways it intersected our lives: the societal injustices of racism; white people's sexual fantasies about black people; the struggle of people such as Dartie's poor white father to help blacks poorer than himself; religious traditions of blacks and whites which did more to divide than unite them; the irony of a white woman from Alabama's notoriously racist Black Belt writing such a novel.

The most important decision we discussed that day was whether we should accept an offer from our Baptist college alma mater in Birmingham to return there to live and teach and raise our soon-to-be-born son. We had decided after the Birmingham church bombing to accept an offer from Florida State or move to a college in Louisville, Kentucky. On the basis of one novel, we placed Alabama back in the running. We would be near parents and siblings we loved, teaching at a Baptist university we understood, helping shape the minds and lives of students we came to adore.

An ironic by-product of our decision to return to Birmingham was friendship with Chris McNair, a professional photographer and Lutheran layman whose beloved eleven-year-old daughter Carol Denise was one of the four children murdered by Ku Klux Klan terrorists in the Sixteenth Street Baptist Church bombing. Later I would contribute to his race for the state legislature where he became one of the first African Americans elected since Reconstruction. I would also lead a seminar in biblical teachings about poverty at Sixteenth Street Baptist Church during a 2009 joint meeting of black Baptists and the Cooperative Baptist Fellowship, a new interracial denomination that former President Jimmy Carter helped organize. Dartie sat beside Carter, who was so impressed with her and her spiffy Sunday hat typical of those that bloomed forth in that biracial setting that he gave her a kiss on the cheek at the end of the service. The photograph made it into the *Birmingham News*, to her considerable embarrassment. Auburn First Baptist Church where we later found a church home welcomed many African American and African members. Some in my Bible class became our close friends, and three became our beloved goddaughters when their father died.

Half a century after our decision to return to Alabama, we had the chance to spend an afternoon answering Nelle's question about why. Dartie—the unofficial timekeeper for long pauses and periods of silence—reckoned that this one broke previous records. Deeply moved that her novel was pivotal to our half-century residence in the state and most of my writing and activism, she uttered what by then was her self-deprecating refrain: "All I did was write a book."

"Perhaps so, Nelle," I replied, "but that book changed our lives forever."

Chapter 8

The Movie

To Kill a Mockingbird HAD A SHADOW LIFE AS A MOVIE. OR PER-
haps the movie had a shadow life as a novel. We could never be
certain if friends' descriptions of the story derived from the novel
or the movie, which are quite different. Whereas Harper Lee
wrote the novel, Horton Foote wrote the movie.

A characteristic Dartie and I valued highly in friends was the
capacity to acknowledge what they did not know. Harper Lee had
proven she could write a book. Despite occasional insinuations
by journalists that she was discourteous, arrogant, and dismissive,
we considered her insecure, tentative, and opinionated. When it
came to making a movie, Nelle did not assume she knew more
than the scriptwriter, director, and producer. At any stage of the
filming, she could have derailed it. Instead, from the sidelines she
mostly cheered the genius of others.

Within her circle of talented friends, it is easy to understand
Nelle's obsequiousness and hesitancy to advance her own ideas.
She was only thirty when a friend took the initiative to connect
her to a literary agent. She was so insecure that she once threw
the early manuscript of *Mockingbird* out the window of her apartment. She also had walked around the block before summoning
the courage to meet her agent for the first time. To that point in

her life, her "published writing" consisted mostly of articles in the University of Alabama humor magazine and student newspaper. She was a law school dropout without a college degree and her only successful employment consisted of clerking for a bookstore and an airline.

Characteristic of her lingering insecurities even in the shadow of her novel's enormous success was her rejection of an offer to write the screenplay. Nor would she interfere with production of the movie. Such intervention almost certainly would have been a disaster because she knew nothing about transforming a novel into a movie or how to retain but alter scenes. Although the studio offered her first option to write the script, she suggested Horton Foote or Alan Pakula instead. The history of cinema and Nelle's reputation were enriched immensely by her concession to what she did not know.

Her cinematic education began at a meeting with producer Alan Pakula, who was two years her junior, a native of the Bronx, and a graduate of Yale University's prestigious theater program. He and a friend, Robert Mulligan, another New York native, and a year older than Nelle, had collaborated on a 1957 movie. They would extend their artistic friendship as producer and director of *Mockingbird* into legendary careers that left no doubt about their pivotal roles in the success of the film. Pakula later directed the award-winning *All the President's Men* and wrote/directed/produced the critically acclaimed *Sophie's Choice*.

In the beginning neither Pakula nor Mulligan was overly enthusiastic about a novel concerning Maycomb, Alabama, a fictional town as remote from their experience as if it had been on Mars. Mulligan described his initial reaction to the novel: "It's about a middle-aged lawyer with two kids. There's no romance, no violence (except off-screen). There's no action. What is there? Where's the story?"

Given that Nelle knew nothing about moviemaking and the director and producer knew nothing about the culture she described, success would depend less on the novel than on the screenplay. Pakula contacted Horton Foote, a Texan who had become an actor, playwright, and television screenwriter living in Nyack, just north of New York City. Although Lee and Horton had arrived in New York from similar Southern towns about the same time, he had not read *Mockingbird* and expressed no interest in adapting the novel into a movie. His wife Lillian, on the other hand, had been an English major at Radcliffe College, was a fan of Eudora Welty and Southern literature, and urged him at least to consider the project: "I know you're going to hiss and holler but I really think you should at least read the novel."

When Foote read *Mockingbird* and learned more about Lee, he realized they had much in common. Wharton, Texas, his hometown, was also a cotton town without paved streets in the 1930s. Its population was also half white, half black. Like Monroeville, it had a history of racial violence and rigid boundaries of race and class. Both towns had a prominent Jewish merchant. Foote's Methodist ancestors had migrated to Texas from Alabama and Georgia. Although he later converted to Christian Science, he described himself as a "Christian Humanist," which also could have described Lee. They shared a Southern sense of place, idiomatic speech patterns, vocabulary, and skill at storytelling. Like Lee, as Foote grew older he became less optimistic about a nation characterized by individualism, hedonism, and injustice. In plays such as *Trip to Bountiful*, he increasingly focused on alienation, loneliness, and family dysfunction. At the same time, he became more spiritually focused on the possibility of repentance, forgiveness, mercy, redemption, and reconciliation. Like Lee he had been a careful student of the Bible. It was, in short, a union made in heaven.

Nevertheless, after reading *Mockingbird* and loving Lee's sense of place which so resonated with his own early life, he resisted dramatizing the novel. He would have to condense three years of book into a single year of screenplay, deleting lots of subplots. But Pakula was unrelenting and urged him at least to meet and talk with Lee.

The evening they met at his home, Lee was in no way shy or reclusive. When describing the evening, Foote told his biographer: "I must say, she sold me. I mean I just loved her; she was a wonderful woman. And I thought, 'Well, I'll enjoy this, if no more than getting to know her.'"

Nelle also liked him instantly. "A great gentleman and so kind," she told us: "I liked him from our first meeting." Then as an afterthought while watching Dartie, she added: "He walked with a cane just like Dartie." On the way home that October evening, I joked, "How does it feel to have Harper Lee compare you favorably to Horton Foote?" "Except for the cane, not bad," she quipped.

Harper had such confidence in Foote after their meeting that she told him to go away until he had finished the script because she did not want to influence what he wrote. According to Foote, she kept her promise except for occasional tips when Foote requested them. When he asked about her characterization of Dill, she told him that her model was childhood friend Truman Capote, which helped Foote flesh out the impish boy in the movie. Whatever their collaboration, Foote insisted, the screenplay "is now my work."

WHAT MADE THEIR COLLABORATION so successful was the similarity of their artistic visions. Nelle explained that a writer need not "shape" fictional characters. They already have a life of their own which the author need only discover and reveal. Foote believed that "remembrance, not nostalgia" is the key to unlocking an imperfect past. He described Atticus Finch as his kind of hero: a man of strong moral convictions; tender; warm; decent; thoughtful; head of a broken family; a relentless believer in personal honor and the essential dignity of all people; someone who upholds Biblical principles of justice but also knows he is imperfect. Like her own father, Nelle rejected religious fundamentalism, judgmentalism, and hypocrisy. The silences and pauses Foote wrote into the script for Boo Radley at the end of the movie, so brilliantly acted by Robert Duvall in his film debut, are why Nelle claimed to be that character.

Following a hiatus in their communication after the film was completed, Foote called one day: "Harper, this is Horton Foote!" Ever ready with a quip, even after a long separation, she said, "Well, do you still have your teeth?" "Yes," he replied, "but I'm gray as a fox." "So am I," she laughed. Decades later he and Mulligan attended her eightieth birthday party, and she attended Foote's ninetieth. She grieved his death as if he had been part of her family.

Although they determined to avoid comment when filming

began in Los Angeles, Lee and Foote were astounded by Pakula and Mulligan's cultural ignorance about small-town Southern life. Foote remembered that their sketch of the Finch home in Monroeville resembled "Tara," the plantation mansion in the film version of *Gone with the Wind*. After considerable good-natured ridicule from Foote and Lee, Pakula found a modest cottage in Pasadena that was about to be demolished for a freeway and moved it to the studio lot. From that point forward, Louise Conner told us, Pakula and Mulligan were so obsessed with authenticity that they flew in collard greens from Alabama for the scene where Calpurnia served them to the Finch family when Walter Cunningham came to dinner. Louise laughed that collards were plentiful in Watts, a black Los Angeles neighborhood consisting mainly of expatriates from the South, and would have cost a lot less to transport.

Both Gregory Peck (Nelle called him "Greg") and his wife, Veronique, adored Harper and Horton, and one of their grandchildren was named in her honor. They also traveled unannounced to Monroeville with Mulligan to meet Nelle's father, study his mannerisms, and observe the town and its inhabitants. Nelle was ambivalent about the visit. Her father was dying of cancer, Peck would be followed by teenagers, and middle-aged women would "swoon" over him. There would be no place to eat in public or any nice hotel. When they left, townsfolk would be mad at her for not telling them beforehand about the visit. The visitors were celebrities whereas she was only Nelle. And she vowed to keep it that way.

HER RELATIONSHIP WITH THE Pecks was not of Hollywood, neither its tinsel nor its sound and fury. When we visited her on

February 2, 2015, I could hardly wait to summarize an interview MSNBC journalist Lawrence O'Brien had with Cecelia Peck, Greg and Veronique's daughter. O'Brien, a long-time acquaintance of the Pecks, asked all the right questions, and Cecelia responded thoughtfully and candidly. I took notes in order to reconstruct the interview for Nelle.

Cecelia was a girl when her father was filming the movie, but the cast mostly functioned like a family. She was allowed on set to watch the child actors who portrayed Scout, Dill, and Jem. In fact, she confided, Nelle became her parents' closest friend.

After the film's release, Cecelia explained that her female school chums told her they wished their fathers were like Atticus Finch. Cecelia remembered Nelle telling her father, "The movie transformed you into Atticus." She then told O'Brien that in some sense that really happened: "He became the father he portrayed on the screen."

When I finished recounting the interview, Nelle sat quietly and reflectively as she often did when our conversations reached the deepest reservoirs of memory. Peck was a rarity, she finally exclaimed, a thoroughly good person who never expressed an unkind word." She then muttered an afterthought: "He was the most cerebral actor of his generation."

I was a lifelong stamp collector, so when the U.S. Postal Service published a commemorative stamp featuring Gregory Peck, I purchased a plate block and had it beautifully framed for her. She displayed it on her wall at The Meadows until her death.

Because Alan Pakula was several years younger than Nelle, we assumed he might be alive. One afternoon, we asked about him. She described his death in 1998 as if it had happened the day before. He had been driving on the Long Island Expressway when a car in front of him ran over a metal pipe on the pavement. The pipe bounced into the air and crashed through Pakula's windshield. He was killed instantly. We were horrified by the details she related of events too painful for more conversation.

WHEN THE MOVIE WAS completed, Nelle loved it. Universal Studio executives did not much like it, but Peck's contract limited their options to withhold distribution.

Some film critics—most notably Roger Ebert in the *Chicago Sun-Times*—agreed with lukewarm Universal Studio executives, embodying later criticism of both novel and film. Ebert panned the movie's "liberal pieties" that go "very easy on the realities of small-town Alabama in the 1960s." His critique of a movie about "more innocent times" that dealt frankly with alleged interracial rape, a white girl's lust for an older black male, poor whites' incest, and a legal lynching, made Dartie and me wonder what movie he had seen.

Ebert ended his review with a hypothetical question that had an historical answer: Can one courageous man and his young child turn away a lynch mob? Actually, yes, they can. And the one courageous man doesn't even need a child. My research and several recent memoirs/biographies of Alabama Methodist ministers detail such events and even incorrectly claim themselves to be Harper Lee's model for Atticus Finch. Courageous law enforcement officials, a judge in Scottsboro, and Judge Horton in Decatur kept the "Scottsboro Boys" alive despite death threats and the termination of some careers. Ultimately all the defendants were released. None was executed. Ebert could have profited from a thorough course about Alabama or even reading a book or two about Southern history.

Probably a preteen child could not have shamed a lynch mob anywhere, as numerous early twentieth-century events outside the South proved. Lynching was mainly the South's shame but not entirely, as the annual reports of locations for such atrocities demonstrated.

Most film critics disagreed with Ebert. They praised the movie, especially Peck's portrayal of Atticus Finch and the score by Elmer Bernstein, which he had played to Pakula over the phone and which Pakula immediately accepted and is now regarded as one of the finest and most memorable scores in film history. The movie won three Academy Awards and three Golden Globes. The Oscar for Best Screenplay Based on Another Medium went to Horton Foote as did the Writers' Guild of America's Best Written American Drama Award. Alan Pakula was inducted into the Producers Guild of America Hall of Fame. The American Film Institute voted *Mockingbird* the fifth-best movie of the twentieth century. In June 2003, coincidentally the month Peck died, the American Film Institute voted his portrayal of Atticus Finch the greatest "hero" role in the history of American cinema. In 2005, the British Film Institute listed it among the fifty films everyone should see before age fourteen. Another poll ranked Peck's portrayal of Atticus among the ten greatest novel-to-movie adaptations of all time.

Perhaps the honor Peck treasured most was A. C. Lee's pocket watch, which Nelle gave to him. She told us that on the evening of the Academy Awards ceremony, Peck had the watch in hand, rubbing it for good luck, when presenter Sophia Loren announced his Academy Award. Brock Peters, who played Tom Robinson, called his role "one of my proudest achievements in life, one of the happiest participations in film or theater I have experienced."

Gregory Peck defined the film's influence on him with a different moral. He was sitting next to a woman at a dinner one evening when she told him that she was fourteen when she first saw the movie, and "it changed my life." Peck continued: "I hear things like that all the time." One day when Nelle was depressed, I quoted Peck's remarks, adding: "Perhaps *Mockingbird* is not the best novel ever written or film ever made; but it may rank number one in changing people's lives, including ours."

Nelle was so enthralled with the film that she agreed to a press conference in Chicago in 1963 celebrating its release. Clever as always despite her unease in such settings, she honed in on a reporter who demonstrated why celebrities often hate journalists who have exhausted all relevant and appropriate questions but keep going anyway: "Don't some people presume the name 'Harper Lee' belongs to a man?" She ended the conference by replying: "Yes! Recently I received an invitation to speak at Yale University, and was told I could stay in the men's dormitory. But I declined that part of the invitation. [Pause] With reluctance!"

To the end of her life, Nelle corrected misconceptions and exaggerations about the book and movie. One afternoon I told her that her childhood acquaintance, Jennings Carter (Truman Capote's cousin), claimed to be the character of Jem in the book and movie. She shot back, "He was no such thing!" On our way home that night Dartie and I agreed that Nelle had made clear that the wise and protective brother in the novel and movie was her beloved brother Ed, a decorated fighter pilot who was shot down in Europe, survived to fly in the Pacific theater, and died of a cerebral hemorrhage after being recalled to service in the Korean War.

Some say that outliving kin and friends is worse than dying young. We were not so sure about that, nor was Nelle. She was as stoical about suffering, declining health, and death as most Southern women. The deaths of her mother, father, brother, two sisters, agent Maurice Crain and editor Tay Hohoff (both in 1970), Alan Pakula (1998), Gregory Peck (2003), Bob Mulligan (2008), and Horton Foote (2009), affected her as profoundly as Dartie's death did me. Whereas I wept and grieved at deaths, Nelle simply retreated into her own private requiem.

Chapter 9

Fame, Privacy, Friends, and Celebrities

ALTHOUGH NELLE WAS NO RECLUSE, SHE WAS ENTIRELY COMFORTable in her own skin. She only occasionally paid attention to how she dressed, wore little if any makeup, did not consider herself pretty, and had grown up preferring golf or "powder-puff" football with other women at the University of Alabama to frivolous socializing or flirtation. She was entirely content reading books. Her social network tended toward people of ideas and independent opinions. She forgave me for being a Baptist because I had written a dozen books about Alabama and the South. Like nearly everyone who knew Dartie, Nelle concluded that having her company was worth tolerating mine.

By any measure, Nelle's most illustrious relationship was not of Alabama or even of New York City, although it did have lots of Alabama connections. Claudia Alta "Lady Bird" Johnson was one year younger than Alice Lee and nearly as long-lived, dying at age ninety-five in 2007. Whether it was Lady Bird's Alabama lineage or her intellectual curiosity about *Mockingbird* and its famous author that triggered the invitation to the White House, we never knew. Whatever the source, the novel's worldwide fame coincided with Lyndon Baines Johnson's (LBJ) vice presidency (1960–1963) and presidency (1963–1968).

The most likely explanation of their friendship is the popularity of the novel written by a woman from Alabama who shared the Johnsons' political ideology. Lady Bird's parents came to Texas from Autauga County, on the northern edge of the Black Belt two counties north of Monroe. Her ancestors had departed from the rich cotton fields near Montgomery for the rich cotton fields of East Texas as part of America's westward movement during hard times in the late nineteenth century. Coincidentally, Horton Foote's ancestors made the same move about the same time.

Lady Bird's mother, descended from an aristocratic family, died in a fall when her daughter was a child. Her father remarried and divorced several times, so stability in her life consisted of summer months spent in Alabama with her aunt and cousins. As the First Lady explained, "Until I was twenty, summertime meant Alabama to me." Although there were picnics beside a creek, watermelon cuttings, and lots of attentive relatives, she did not learn "social graces" such as small talk, dancing, and the art of courtship. As a result, she was shy, nervous in conversations, bookish, and independent-minded, which would have been a fair description of Harper Lee at a similar age. Lady Bird attended a summer session at the University of Alabama but then transferred to a small Episcopal woman's college in Texas. After completing its preparatory curriculum, she debated whether to return to the University of Alabama or enter the University of Texas. Fields of bluebonnets blooming near the campus the day of her springtime visit to Austin sealed the deal.

A student so smart and socially insecure that she sometimes

slacked off studying in order not to be first in her classes, she nonetheless majored in history before taking a second major in journalism with honors. Not only did she excel in school, she also managed the Johnson family finances after her marriage to Lyndon in 1934. Her father helped fund Johnson's first congressional campaign, and she shrewdly invested in radio and television stations that made the Johnsons millionaires while promoting his political ambitions.

From early life, LBJ had an eye for the ladies, according to Nelle—a not unusual trait among Texas or Alabama men or men in general. I couldn't resist the temptation to joke that despite Nelle's exemption of me in her generalization, I had an eye for her on the rare occasions when she behaved. That resulted in much laughter and some uncomplimentary comments about men in general from both Nelle and Dartie.

Like his wife's ancestors, Lyndon's came from Alabama. His paternal grandfather, Samuel Ealy Johnson, was born in 1838 in Wedowee, only some forty miles south of where I grew up.

Like many bright women married to philandering husbands, Lady Bird carved out a separate identity. Presidential historians have noted that she was an important influence in the Johnson administration, especially pushing for stronger civil rights legislation. Johnson knew that was politically risky at a time when a large portion of the Democratic Party's electoral base was in the segregated South. Accurately anticipating the Republican "Southern Strategy" of the late 1960s that would alter the terrain of American politics for generations, Johnson only reluctantly heeded her instincts and those of his closest advisors. Lady Bird not only operated in an independent sphere of American politics during her husband's presidency, she actively campaigned for him in the Deep South during the 1964 presidential race and referred to their years in the White House as "our presidency." She privately critiqued his news conferences and public appearances, even grading his speeches. He had symptoms of bipolar disorder and needed constant affirmation when depressed, which she provided.

Although Lyndon often criticized Lady Bird's meddling, she was more important to his presidency than any White House staffer. When he threatened to fire his longtime advisor, Walter Jenkins, who had been outed as being gay, she defended Jenkins.

Lady Bird was famous in her own public role as conservationist and beautifier of America, including passage of the Highway Beautification Act that provided for planting wildflowers along interstate highways and removing billboards. She also supported arguably the most liberal domestic agenda in American history: Medicare and Medicaid; the Civil Rights Act of 1964 and the Voting Rights Act of 1965; federal preschool education; and significant environmental legislation.

We never asked when or how their friendship began, but the Vice President and Lady Bird invited Nelle to visit their Texas home and speak to students. After LBJ assumed the presidency, the Johnsons invited her to a glitzy White House dinner. The president—standing six feet four inches and weighing a good deal more than two hundred pounds—could be a formidable presence moving from table to table like a bull roaming a pasture on his Texas hill country ranch. Nelle described him as "dominating" in height, heft, demeanor, and voice, socially towering over every function she attended.

Sometime in the early stages of their friendship, the President mentioned that his paternal grandfather had been born in the Appalachian foothills of Randolph County in east central Alabama. Like Nelle's, Johnson's paternal grandfather had fought in the Confederate Army. I resisted the temptation to tell Nelle that he was also a Baptist.

She and the Johnsons obviously connected along the Alabama axis of author, novel, racial enlightenment, and dislike for demagogue George Wallace. Johnson appointed Nelle to the National Council on the Arts and invited her to White House events. Nelle traveled to them from New York City by train, often returning late at night. For the occasions, she dressed stylishly, an impressive looking woman when she made an effort to impress people. At one White House affair she was seated at a table with Robert Oppenheimer, the famous nuclear physicist, whom she described as a fascinating dinner companion. We imagined that he might have said the same thing about her. LBJ became her favorite American president, although she always liked Lady Bird best and regarded her as a personal friend. The fact that her self-declared favorite president became an activist champion of civil rights is a revealing insight into her own legacy.

IN ADDITION TO POLITICAL celebrities, she had lots of literary and arts friends. Although Truman Capote and his circle monopolized her early years in New York, his eclipse made way for successful Alabama writers such as Diane McWhorter, Fannie Flagg, and Wayne Greenhaw. Other writers occasionally arrived at The Meadows during one of our visits with Nelle, and the result was always entertaining and revelatory. The day Rick Bragg received the Harper Lee prize, he stopped by to pay homage. A popular journalist, memoirist, and humorist, he mentioned the name of a mutual literary acquaintance whom he identified as "influential and interesting." Nelle translated his meaning into one of her metaphors: "She was the straw that stirred the liquor."

On another visit, we shared news we had just heard that movie star Charlton Heston had died. As teenagers Dartie and I had seen Heston's movie portrayal of Moses, which seemed to have lasted as long as the Egyptian captivity, the desert wanderings, and the conquest of the Promised Land. I asked Nelle if she had met him. "Only once, "she replied, "at one of Truman's parties." She laughed, "The arrogant son-of-a-bitch couldn't decide if he was Moses or God."

One day we arrived early in the afternoon when Nelle was watching television. She told me to turn "that thing off." Aware of her worsening macular degeneration, I asked if she watched television often. She replied that she had difficulty hearing it and generally didn't like what she did hear. We had just returned from lectures in the U.K., so I told her about an incident we had in London's Bloomsbury district at an antiquarian bookstore that was a favorite of hers. I had taken several books to the counter for purchase when I saw a sign next to the cash register which read: "'I consider television quite educational. Every time someone turns one on, I go into another room and read a book.'—Groucho Marx"

She laughed, and I remembered that she had told us one afternoon that her favorite movies growing up in the 1930s were Marx Brothers comedies. I asked if she had met Groucho. To our surprise, she said that he had attended the cast party for the release of

Mockingbird. Apparently he was a friend of the Pecks, who invited him. Although the theater was dark, light from the screen was sufficient for her to see Marx's face during the dramatic scene near the end of the movie when Reverend Sykes, the African American preacher, tells Scout, "Miss Jean Louise, stand up. Your father's passing." Nelle noticed a tear rolling down Marx's cheek, a not uncommon reaction as the courtroom drama mounts.

By the end of the movie, when the theater lights came up, Marx had regained his composure. Nelle fell in line behind him as friends congratulated Peck for his brilliant portrayal of Atticus Finch. She noticed that Marx began to mimic mannerisms from his films, chewing on a cigar which he bounced up and down with his teeth and wiggling his eyebrows up and down. When he reached the theater exit where Peck was standing, Nelle anticipated some warm words of tribute. Instead, Marx told the star, "Better luck on your next case, Greg!" The satirical witticism so discombobulated her that she neglected to introduce herself to Marx or tell him how much she had enjoyed his movies while growing up.

Among celebrities she never knew but who wanted to know her, we ranked the Obamas highest. Given the frequency with which President Barack Obama quoted *Mockingbird* and his award to her of the Presidential Medal of the Arts, we regretted that after her stroke the prospect of the arduous train ride to the White House dissuaded her from going. What a treat it would have been to see our favorite author receive the award in person from one of our favorite presidents.

WE ALSO WERE NEVER able to connect Nelle with Mary Ward

Brown of Perry County at the other end of the Black Belt. Born in the tiny hamlet of Hamburg, which no longer exists, Mary T, as she was called, was an American master of the short story who was not "discovered" until she was up in years. She won the prestigious Pen/Hemingway Prize for best first work of fiction, the Hillsdale Award from the Fellowship of Southern Writers, the Lillian Smith Book Award, and was chosen among twenty American writers for a cultural exchange with a similar number of Russian writers during the short-lived years of *Glasnost* (healing) between the two nations.

Dartie made a celebratory meal in honor of Mary T's ninetieth birthday and return from Russia and New York City. Slow talking, soft-voiced, and melodic in the honey-toned consonants of the Black Belt, Mary T received our accolades and Dartie's food with equal delight. In a pensive mood following a whirlwind season of travel to places she had never been, and acknowledging fame she had not imagined, she greeted us with wisdom we never forgot: "This fame business will kill you!" Nelle did not express the sentiment in those words, but that is what she also believed.

Nelle considered fame among life's paradoxes. She fully understood that some of the most famous people have also been among the loneliest and most unhappy. Of the examples we could have chosen to discuss, J. D. Salinger was obvious. After achieving literary fame for *Catcher in the Rye*, he moved from his apartment on East 57th Street, not far from where Nelle lived, to the small hamlet of Cornish, New Hampshire. Like her, he published little after his best-selling novel. Also like her, he continued to write and file manuscripts away (her "The Reverend"). Describing this phase of his life, he wrote: "It is my rather subversive opinion that a writer's feelings of anonymity-obscurity are the second most valuable property on loan to him during his working years." Popular magazines increasingly referred to him, as to Nelle, as "reclusive." He wrote his eighteen-year-old future mistress warning her about the perils of fame, which she soon learned for herself.

Nelle, like many famous writers, assumed that her only reliable friends were the ones from before fame. She particularly distrusted journalists and biographers, for good reason, as it turned out. I had written multiple biographies and a book about Southern poor whites before we knew Nelle. Fortunately, the biographies concerned obscure Florida politicians or Christian missionaries. When we came to know the Lee family, I was known almost exclusively as an Alabama historian. Had I not been that, I am convinced there never would have been a Harper Lee-Flynt friendship, despite winsome Dartie and our validation by Louise and Alice.

DURING THE YEARS OF our friendship with Nelle, we witnessed both the cynicism and accuracy of her distrust. When one reporter badgered her with requests for an interview, she dismissed him with a two-word rejection written on the rumpled letter he sent: "Go away!" His subsequent disquisition on the meaning of the two words was a masterpiece of irrelevance.

Nelle's accounts of an acquaintance who secretly recorded conversations with a hidden digital device and reporters who, abetted sometimes by Monroeville residents, invaded her room at the Meadows, sent chills down our spines. A reporter for a London newspaper—aided by a Monroeville accomplice who tracked down Nelle's room number by calling her exercise therapist without revealing the reason—barged into her room demanding an interview from a woman trapped in a wheelchair. After that violation, she could not leave her door open, and the staff fabricated a fake name plate for it. False allegations of elder abuse against her attorney were followed by criminal investigations and rumors of dementia. Monroeville residents divided into camps, some fiercely guarding her privacy, others lusting for their two minutes of fame on national television. Journalist Cynthia Tucker told me that only Nelle's mysterious and intensely private persona and international fame kept Monroeville economically afloat.

Her local fame was centered in the wonderful little museum in the iconic (though not particularly historic) courthouse on the town square. The museum generated considerable revenue, especially in the springtime when an excellent amateur cast performed the *Mockingbird* play in the courthouse. During our trips to carry Auburn students to the play, or even occasionally to lecture to audiences before performances, we found local hotels filled, the local bookstore busy, and restaurants overflowing. Visitors came from every state and from abroad. They spent considerably more money on lodging, food, drink, and souvenirs than on the modestly priced theater tickets. Local folks were as courteous and helpful as small-town Alabamians tend to be toward visitors. Then a 2014 spat over royalties paid for *Mockingbird* souvenirs sparked a lawsuit and lots of local grievances.

Dartie and I had grown up in similar small towns where such feuds had been divisive and hurtful. Nelle fumed in her tiny apartment about what she referred to as the town's exploitation of her fame and intellectual property. Or, as she uttered to us in summary of what was happening, "Same damn town and same damned people as in *Mockingbird*!"

Local folks refused to believe that Nelle's deceased saintly sister Alice would have done such a thing and blamed Tonja Carter, who had been chosen by Alice to succeed her as head of the law firm. Tonja's family had moved to Monroeville from the Midwest. After a divorce and remarriage to Patrick Carter, a relative of Truman Capote, she had become Alice's law clerk/secretary. She and Patrick also converted to Catholicism. Alice helped Tonja attend law school and groomed her to take over Alice's legal practice. In small Southern towns there is no finer villain in a local soap opera than a "Damn Yankee," however remote William Tecumseh Sherman's plundering "March to the Sea" through Georgia may have been. A boycott of the Carters' excellent restaurant on the Monroeville square temporarily closed it.

Six months later, Nelle remained peeved. That was also the context for her answer to my question about her favorite book of the Bible: "Exodus, because they are leaving."

We had "no dog in this fight," as Alabamians like to tell each other, and we knew enough about wounds to both winners and losers to remain bystanders trying to understand everyone's grievances. When Dartie consoled Nelle by explaining that loss of privacy almost always is a byproduct of fame, she found no comfort in that explanation. Six decades earlier she had written in *Watchman*: "I can't explain it [but] I'd go stark raving mad living in Maycomb." Now life was imitating art.

Expanding her grievances that same year, she complained about a forthcoming book about her. Alice attributed the disagreement to Nelle's deafness and tendency to answer "Yes" to any question whether or not she understood it. Journalists were also increasingly portraying her as suffering from dementia, based on reports by locals who had absolutely no contact with her.

One day when we arrived, she was furious and repeated for what seemed the hundredth time that anyone who claimed to have her permission to write about her lied. We spent the rest of the afternoon telling her stories about our granddaughter and her namesake until her rage subsided.

Cammie Plummer Cowan, her longtime Mobile friend, told us the most chilling story about Nelle's loss of autonomy. Before the stroke, Nelle had scheduled a minor surgery in Mobile. Cammie decided to "look after her," a duty Nelle had performed for Cammie decades earlier in New York. Cammie was appalled when a hospital anesthetist asked Nelle to autograph a book after she had already relinquished her eyeglasses and been hooked up to a drip. Nelle reluctantly signed the book. The worst was yet to come. As Nelle was waking up in recovery, the same woman presented her son's paperback copy for a signature. Cammie "went berserk" (to use her phrase) about the unprofessional conduct and threatened to file a complaint with hospital administrators. She also described Nelle's post-operative assessment: "Well, I did think it was sort of unprofessional. I wondered where the hospital staff kept getting books. Does everyone on the hospital staff walk around with a book all the time?" Later she giggled to Cammie that she was so groggy from the anesthesia that "they'll never be able to sell those books because the autographs were unrecognizable."

SUCH INCIDENTS BECAME SO frequent that she usually forgot them, but she could not forget the assassination of John Lennon a few blocks from her New York City apartment. That event made a lasting impression which she described for us one afternoon. Lennon's murderer carried a copy of *Catcher in the Rye* and was obsessed with celebrities who were "phonies," as Salinger's character Holden Caulfield believed all adults were. She told us that the attempted assassin of President Ronald Reagan also was obsessed with the Salinger novel and cited it in his defense. We knew Nelle enjoyed reading true crime books, but these events unnerved her.

Beyond regretting her anxiety, we did not take such threats seriously until one afternoon when she told a story. The details were garbled but the event harrowing. A man rang the doorbell. When Nelle opened the door, he demanded she autograph his copy of *Mockingbird*. She extemporaneously concocted one of her most convincing stories, shouting that the Monroe County sheriff lived across the street (not true) and she would have him arrested if he bothered her again. Given her anger and physicality before her stroke, arrest might have been his best available option. He departed amidst a barrage of threats and insults and never returned. But the incident was sufficiently vivid that she repeated the story several times. Rarely did she permit such a presumption anywhere, but certainly not from a stranger invading her hometown space.

One afternoon, I asked why she had stopped making public appearances. She did not cite that incident or any like it, only six words: "Didn't need to. Didn't want to." Vintage Harper Lee. Our minds filled in the blank spaces. In her own way, and independent of other writers, Nelle had concluded that fame brought as much pain as satisfaction. Perhaps no public adulation justifies the discomfort private people experience when forced into public spaces.

One event came close though. She described the efforts of her

Mobile ophthalmologist—a University of Notre Dame graduate who treated her macular degeneration—to persuade her to accept an honorary degree from his alma mater. She finally consented to accept the degree and present brief remarks to the graduating class. Realizing how unprecedented her appearance was, and having read her novel in middle or high school, the graduates had a surprise for her when she was introduced. The entire class rose, each graduate holding high a copy of *To Kill a Mockingbird*, and cheered. Unlike uncounted honors and awards at other times and in other places, she never forgot that one.

Of the many facts and anecdotes describing Nelle's fame which could have been included in her February 21, 2016, obituary in London's *Sunday Times*, we were glad the writer chose that one. We knew Nelle also would have been pleased.

Chapter 10

The Lost Final Book, 'The Reverend'

In 1963, at the peak of her fame, a reporter asked Nelle if the successes of the novel and the movie "will spoil Harper Lee?" She replied with a quip she often used at press conferences: "She's too old!" At age thirty-seven then, her answer was a disingenuous diversion. She had plenty of time left. His follow-up question about what would be her next book elicited a more authentic reply: "I'm scared!" Of course, she was referring to the public expectations about every successful novelist's next book. But interpreted retrospectively, her answer is chilling.

We never learned exactly what drew Nelle to the Willie Maxwell murder case, although, in some strange and undefinable way, crime and violence have always occupied the fringes of human conduct and the center of human curiosity. Her beloved King James Bible contained plenty of both, as did *King Lear*, her favorite Shakespearean drama. Even in childhood she was drawn to novels about those subjects. Part of the attraction of Truman Capote's invitation to join him in Garden City, Kansas, to research the Clutter murders was her fascination with the underside of human conduct. A few years later, while Truman exulted in the fame of *In Cold Blood*, Nelle scrutinized clippings and documents about a bizarre murder in Alexander City, Alabama.

The small county seat in Tallapoosa County is in the Appalachian foothills where one of America's first gold strikes occurred. The Reverend Willie Maxwell was at the center of the story. A handsome African American with a thin mustache, he was physically imposing, nearly six and a half feet tall. The former Marine had served in the chemical division and had been trained in compounds that could kill without leaving a trace.

Maxwell was the sort of man whites respected, owning a pulpwood business that employed uneducated black men to wield chain saws and load logs on his truck. He was also a bivocational Baptist preacher, a common pattern among both black and white congregations in the rural and small-town South where churches of less than a hundred members were common and pastors depended on income from secular employment. As in most places, church attendance appealed more to women than men, so his parishioners consisted mainly of females. Whether single or married, many women found the handsome, prosperous, well-dressed, charismatic "preacher-man" attractive.

In 1968, Maxwell's wife, Mary Lou, was found dead in what first appeared to be an automobile accident. As the incident unfolded, Willie Maxwell was charged with murder. He hired Tom Radney as his attorney. Tom, an acquaintance of mine in the Democratic Party, had been an influential state senator until he left office in the 1970s. He foresaw that Republicans would win control of the Alabama legislature after white voters abandoned the Democrats—as Lyndon Johnson had predicted when he signed the Voting Rights Act.

Radney was charming, well-liked in Coosa and Tallapoosa counties which he represented in the legislature, and brilliant in and out of court. He held fish fries in addition to more formal and better lubricated functions to which he invited a mix of the textile workers and businessmen he might need to argue to on juries. When outside corporate attorneys came to town to test Tom's skill in the courtroom, they usually departed with diminished reputations.

Maxwell's next-door neighbor, Dorcas Anderson, was scheduled to be the state's star witness. But when time approached for the trial, she claimed not to recall her earlier statements concerning his frightened wife or the Reverend's absence the night of the "accident." In fact, in her revised testimony, she provided him an alibi for the night of the murder. Prosecutors were outraged at what they considered to be witness tampering and perjury. After charges were dismissed, Radney sued Beneficial Standard Life Insurance Company on behalf of Maxwell, who regularly purchased life insurance policies on relatives. Such insurance companies made large profits by selling policies for a few dollars a month to working-class black and white families. I knew this part of the story well because when I was a young boy, my father sold such policies door-to-door in north Alabama. The companies made money because most policy owners did not murder their wives.

Not only was Tom Radney my friend, so was John Denson, the attorney he faced off with in one of the civil cases that followed Maxwell's acquittal for murder. I had come to know John as a respected Auburn University trustee, a prominent Methodist layman, and a devotee of Harper Lee. In fact, Denson's father had served with Nelle's father in the state legislature during the 1920s. John once loaned me a sketch book that included profiles of the two men to share with Nelle, to her delight.

While preparing his defense of Beneficial Standard, John had interviewed Dorcas Anderson. She told him that Maxwell's wife was terrified of him, that unidentified women frequently called their house, and the night of his wife's death Maxwell left in plenty of time to have committed the murder.

After Radney won Maxwell's case against Beneficial Standard, Maxwell walked over to Denson, put a hand on his shoulder, and told him: "Brother Denson, you said some awfully mean things about me in this trial, but I have asked the Lord to forgive you, and He said He would, and I do too. Just go and sin no more!" Maxwell's arrogance was unsettling, and John was relieved when the insurance company paid two ensuing questionable death settlements involving Maxwell's relatives rather than confront Maxwell and Radney again in court. John told me that African Americans he tried to interview for the trials wouldn't even let him on their porches, describing Maxwell as the "voodoo man."

While dining later at a nearby marina, Denson recognized a black waiter who had attended the trial and attempted to talk with him. The man confirmed that black folks in Alex City considered Maxwell a "voodoo doctor" who could cast spells, then he quickly disappeared into the kitchen.

A year after Maxwell's acquittal for murder, he and Dorcas Anderson married. Amazingly, life insurance companies continued to write policies as other Maxwell relatives mysteriously continued to die. John assured me there was something "really spooky" about everything surrounding Maxwell. When subsequently contacted by insurance companies foolish enough to continue writing policies, John declined to take the cases.

MAXWELL DIED AS HE lived. Following five mysterious family deaths, one of his in-laws, Robert Lewis Burns, murdered Maxwell in front of three hundred people in a funeral home chapel on June 18, 1977. Given that there were so many eyewitnesses, the verdict in Burns's subsequent murder trial seemed a foregone conclusion. Such an assumption reckoned without the skill of Burns's attorney, Tom Radney, who may have been even better at voodoo with a Tallapoosa County jury than Willie Maxwell was with a strangled chicken hung on his porch. Still, a lawyer defending the murderer of a man for whom he had earlier won an acquittal for murder was strange even for Alexander City.

Jim Earnhardt was a young reporter for the *Alexander City Outlook* at the time. Years later, he recalled for me the pandemonium in the funeral home chapel the day Maxwell was shot. People trampled each other rushing out the door. Some leapt out windows. Earnhardt also described his interview with a member of the all-white jury that voted to acquit Burns. When asked how the juror could find Burns not guilty of shooting an unarmed Baptist preacher sitting on a pew in a chapel with three hundred witnesses, the answer combined amazement that the question had to be asked, with working-class Alabama commonsense about justice: "Some people just ought to be shot!"

Nelle read about the case and was intrigued. Compared to the twists and turns of the Maxwell case, the Clutter murders in Kansas seemed transparent and uncomplicated. She was soon on her way to Alexander City to conduct interviews and do research. Her apprenticeship in Kansas had left her well rehearsed in how to conduct such interviews. But, as she soon discovered, Garden City, Kansas, was quite different from Alexander City, Alabama.

By chance, Nelle's niece owned a motel in the small city. Nelle spent months there while she interviewed anyone who would talk with her, including Burns, Maxwell's killer. Lawyer Tom Radney himself proved a charming and cooperative source. The Radneys found Nelle to be witty, sociable, and a quick study about legal matters. After Nelle returned to New York, Radney grew impatient as time passed and he received no reports about progress on a book, which presumably was why she had been in town. Nelle finally sent four pages of manuscript, but there would be no further sighting of a book finished or in progress.

One Sunday afternoon while Dartie and I were visiting Louise Conner in Eufaula, we were sharing stories about translations of *Mockingbird* when she asked if we would like to see some of them. We had no idea she had stored away first editions in various languages, and we expressed keen interest. We walked into a bedroom where she had dozens of neatly shelved translations.

As we returned to the porch, I mentioned rumors that Nelle had written another book about a black preacher and a series of murders. "Oh, yes," Louise replied, steering us into her dining room where she pointed to the center table and said, "Nelle wrote 'The Reverend' sitting at that table while helping me care for my husband who was dying." (Her son Ed thought Nelle actually wrote most of the manuscript in a small room Louise had used as an office.)

We were stunned by that news. And we asked no questions about the fate of the manuscript, whether Nelle still had it, whether she had completed or revised it in New York City, or whether it might soon be published.

Harper Lee was still alive and, so far as we knew, in good health. We had met her only once, at the previously mentioned Eufaula history and heritage festival. We thought questions about an unknown manuscript would have been presumptuous and meddling, or even worse, would have been seen as curiosity about the famous sister rather than our utterly fascinating friend, Louise Conner. However, we later learned that once when Nelle was visiting Cammie Plummer, her then-husband P. D. East had said he "might as well play the bastard" and ask if she was writing another book. "Yes," she had replied, "about a murder in north Alabama." In fact, Alexander City was in central Alabama, but to someone from Monroeville, it would have seemed "north."

Four decades later on April 5, 2015, Nelle spun out for us the story of the Maxwell murders, his three wives, the name of his killer, even the name of the reporter who covered the case. That conversation resulted from the most serendipitous set of circumstances. I had just completed a long phone call with a physician in Eufaula. His son was a member of the Pilgrims Sunday school class I taught in Auburn. The son told me one Sunday morning that his father wanted to talk with me. I provided my phone number. His father called on April 19, two weeks before our conversation about the Maxwell case with Nelle.

The good doctor explained that Louise Conner was one of his patients and had called to ask permission for Harper Lee to contact him about some neurological problems. Assuming that the fiercely private novelist was experiencing some personal medical problems, he scheduled a phone call while he began researching various mental and emotional conditions that might arise in their conversation. But when Nelle called, their long conversation concerned not her own health but the effects of certain chemicals on the brain, which ones could be lethal and not easily traced. Mystified by the entire conversation, he finally concluded that she was working on a new book, although he knew no details about the Maxwell case.

A few years later I speculated about various reasons why her book, if completed as Louise claimed it had been, was never published. Coincidentally, an Auburn graduate student living in rural Tallapoosa County had enrolled in my Southern history class. We became friends as she wrote fine local history books. One day as we talked, she told me about a new project, the Maxwell murders. She was aware of rumors that Harper Lee had written a novel about the bizarre events. The next time we talked, my former student had abandoned the project. The Reverend Maxwell's many relatives were not only uncooperative, they were menacing. Intimations of voodoo and threats that bad things happened to people snooping around and asking questions made her nervous. Then a Maxwell relative who lived across a rural road from her, and who owned a fierce guard dog whose only restraint seemed to be a chain link fence, warned her not to pursue the topic.

THE SECOND TIME WE hesitantly mentioned the Maxwell case to Nelle, she was entirely unresponsive. It was the closest we witnessed of a complete memory lapse. On the way home, Dartie and I agreed that perhaps her "memory problem" consisted less of what she had forgotten than of what she still remembered.

Years later we asked Nelle's executor Tonja Carter about the missing manuscript, assuming she might know its fate. She told us that while Alice was still heading the law firm, a doctoral student writing a dissertation about Harper Lee had asked about rumors of a book concerning murders in Alabama. According to Tonja, Alice acknowledged that Nelle had written such a book but doubted that it would ever be published because of threatened lawsuits by parties to the complex events.

My mind processed the conversations in the context of a similar threat by Monroeville's Boulware family, whose troubled son was reputedly the model for Boo Radley in *Mockingbird*. Writers are often threatened with suits and harassed, so I assumed the missing draft about the Maxwell murders could be explained by Nelle's telephone conversation with my physician acquaintance, followed by intimidation, threats of legal action, and perhaps even her fear of violence by the Maxwell family. Ed Conner told me years later that threats had frightened Nelle so badly that she swore Louise Conner to secrecy, warning of possible violence to the entire Lee family.

According to the Radneys, when they flew to New York City trying to recoup documents Tom had loaned to Nelle, she was drinking heavily. On several occasions when I spoke in Alex City, Radney's wife asked if I could help retrieve the materials. I declined to become entangled in such private matters. The papers were finally returned to the Radneys.

In *Furious Hours*, the fascinating book about the Maxwell murders, Tom Radney, and Harper Lee, author Casey Cep speculates that something more elemental explains why Harper Lee never finished "The Reverend": by then both her talented agent, Maurice Crain, and her superb editor, Tay Hohoff, were dead. Hohoff had played a pivotal role in transforming a deeply flawed initial manuscript into *Mockingbird*.

According to Tonja Carter, the endlessly trusting Alice Lee reached into the bookshelves above her desk, retrieved the manuscript of "The Reverend," and handed it to an aspiring doctoral student with the promise of its return when he had finished reading it. The student never returned it.

I hope that somewhere in America there is a guilt-ridden English teacher (or more likely a failed graduate student) who preserves yet another unpublished fragment of Harper Lee's literary heritage, perhaps the best of all, and will someday share it with the world.

Chapter 11

Life Derailed

IN THE EARLY SPRING OF 2007, NELLE AWOKE IN THE NIGHT AT her Manhattan apartment feeling unwell. She could not move her left arm or leg. She knew she had suffered a stroke. When she tried to stand up, she fell to the floor and could not move. Her phone was on the far side of the bed. She lay on the floor for hours in the critical immediate aftermath of a stroke. Finally, harnessing her remaining strength from decades of vigorous walking across Manhattan, she pulled herself back onto the bed and fell into exhausted sleep. The following afternoon she was awakened by a ringing telephone. Her friend Susan Colvin, who lived nearby, notified Diane McWhorter, their mutual friend from Birmingham, and the two rushed to Nelle's apartment. The door was locked, and by the time the building superintendent brought a key, Nelle was in the bathroom cleaning up. An emergency crew arrived about the same time and transported her to Mount Sinai Hospital. McWhorter had the foresight to admit her under "Nelle Lee," thus preventing an intrusive and sensational journalistic event.

After three weeks at Mount Sinai, Nelle's insurance required that she be transferred to a rehabilitation facility. Tom Carruthers, a Birmingham attorney and family acquaintance, suggested she be moved to Lakeshore Rehabilitation Hospital south of Birmingham in the Homewood suburb.

Tom may have been one of the few people in America who could have successfully protected Harper Lee's secret for nearly a year. For six decades he had been a partner in Bradley Arant Rose and White, the city's most prestigious law firm. In fact, it was rated first among all American firms in the percentage of its attorneys listed in "Best Lawyers in America." Like Alice Lee, he specialized in tax law. Those who only casually knew the unpretentious attorney were unaware of his pedigree: magna cum laude undergraduate of Princeton, J.D. from Yale where he won the prestigious Thurman Arnold Appellate Prize, and a listing among the best American attorneys.

Like Alice, Tom was a genuinely decent, ethical, and progressive attorney. He chaired the trustee boards of Children's Hospital, Lakeshore Foundation, Birmingham Legal Aid Board, and the governor's Tax Reform Task Force, where I came to know him while facilitating settlement of a successful lawsuit against the state's inequitable funding of public education for African Americans, rural poor whites, and disabled children. Unwilling to fly because of motion sickness, Nelle traveled to Birmingham by train, accompanied by her then agent, Sam Pinkus. On May 13— coincidentally Mother's Day that year—Tom called us, swore us to secrecy, and summarized the awful events of the past month.

Nelle had suffered a stroke. She would be at Lakeshore for rehabilitation for months. She would be bored and lonely. Alice was nearly three hours' driving time away and was in her mid nineties. Only Nelle's closest friends from New York and a few Alabamians selected by Tom, Alice, and Nelle herself would be notified and allowed to visit. Tom told us the fake name under which Nelle had been admitted and the name of the Lakeshore official who would screen anyone who asked about the mysterious patient. Another Lakeshore official would accompany us to her room. Nurses and physical therapists were sworn to secrecy, probably under threat of dismissal given that apparently no reporters found out what had happened.

After Nelle's unhappiness in Mt. Sinai and temporary loneliness at Lakeshore, she contrived a fictional identity and alternative reality. One of her favorite movie stars was Humphrey Bogart, and her favorite film (other than *Mockingbird*, of course) was *Casablanca*. Thus the name she chose for her secret visitors was "The Usual Suspects," from a line in that movie. Her anonymity, secret society, fake name, convoluted plot, stealth visitors, physical challenges, whispers and rumors, potential outing by some publicity-seeking Lakeshore employee or persistent reporter—all turned an ordeal into a fanciful half-year of intrigue and hijinks.

She informed me that "The Usual Suspects" were all females, and I was not welcomed (though she relented). Alice, Tonja, Dartie, Susan Colvin, Diane McWhorter, Birmingham attorney Susan Doss, and University of Alabama icon Cathy Randall, among other illuminati, relieved the tedious, strenuous, and monotonous physical routine of rehab. For their efforts, they received pins to wear on their blue T-shirts identifying them as members of the royal but not so ancient order of "The Usual Suspects."

I had just retired from forty years of university teaching, and we were regularly visiting my widowed mother, who lived north of Birmingham. On our return trips, we began stopping at Lakeshore several times a month. When casting about for some way to relieve Nelle's boredom, we thought of our new CD player and a collection of books we listened to while traveling. On our next visit, we took the player and three of our favorite books: Jane Austen's *Pride and Prejudice*, Eudora Welty reading her own short story "Why I Live at the P.O.," and British comedian John Cleese's oral interpretation of C. S. Lewis's *Screwtape Letters*. Nelle was jubilant. She offered profuse gratitude which we dismissed as typical Southern good manners. During subsequent years, we learned that Austen, Welty, and Lewis were indeed three of her favorite writers. Some will consider this coincidence or serendipity. At that low point in her life, we considered it divine providence.

On our next visit, Dartie substituted homemade chocolate brownies for CDs. She received permission from hospital staff for the treat and as we entered the room, she asked Nelle if she liked chocolate. As Nelle reached for the container, she responded, "Is the Pope Catholic?" Before the CDs and brownies, we had just been friends of Alice and Louise. That day Dartie's brownies were our portal from acquaintanceship to friendship. On our trip home that afternoon, Dartie and I discussed how sad it must be to hold everyone at arm's length for fear they were curiosity seekers, journalists, or aspiring biographers.

Nelle slowly settled into a routine of physical therapy, hospital food, and occasional visits from old friends and new ones. Her creative sense of humor blossomed, and her mind spun out new adventures like "The Usual Suspects." She enjoyed some visitors more than others. She described the bishop of one denomination as "coming early and staying late," leaving only after a feisty nurse interrupted to ask Nelle if she needed to use the bathroom.

On the following visit, we talked to Nelle at length about

Eudora Welty. We considered Welty to be America's master of the short story. I told Nelle that I had autographed copies of nearly all Welty's first editions. This surprised her. I shared the first of many Welty-related stories.

In 1992, I served as Eudora Welty Scholar of Southern Studies at Millsaps College, a fine Methodist liberal arts school in Jackson, Mississippi, not far south of where I was born in Pontotoc. The best perk of that semester other than getting to know Miss Welty was proximity to the office of English professor Suzanne Marrs, whose friendship with Welty made possible a splendid biography of the great lady and established a pattern for our relationship with Nelle: first, be her friend; then, respect her privacy; write about her only after her death.

One autumn evening, Dartie and I took Welty to dinner. During the conversation, we mentioned Harper Lee. We told Welty that we had met her once when she spoke at an event in Eufaula where one of her sisters lived. Although we did not know Lee, we knew her sisters Alice and Louise. Welty's curiosity about the intensely private Monroeville novelist matched ours.

On the spur of the moment, I volunteered to ask Louise Conner if she would invite Harper Lee to spend an afternoon with Eudora Welty while home for the holidays. We offered to chauffeur Welty to Monroeville or Eufaula. To our surprise, Welty seemed intrigued.

We called Louise Conner, who contacted her sister, who not only agreed but, according to Louise, seemed genuinely excited at the prospect. We were beyond excitement. Just imagine being, quiet as mice but taking in every word, in the same room with two towering figures of Southern literature.

When the fall semester ended and we returned to Auburn, Louise called to tell us that Harper had reneged. Whether from inconvenience, timidity, or panic, we never learned. Years later, Nelle claimed to remember nothing about the discussions. We told her that Welty's awe at spending a day with Harper Lee was certainly as daunting as Harper's anxiety about meeting Welty.

TOWARD THE END OF the six months of rehab, Nelle had progressed sufficiently for us to take her out for dinner. We correctly assumed that a late afternoon meal afforded our best chance of anonymity. She was underdressed as usual, wearing loose-fitting pedal pushers, a white T-shirt, and tennis shoes. After months of hospital grub, she swooned at the food. When the check arrived, I offered my credit card. Lowering her head and looking embarrassed, she blurted out another of her aphorisms: "I don't have a penny or a purse to put it in." Our friendship was of too recent vintage for me to say any of the things I was thinking: taking Harper Lee to dinner can't be measured in dollars; if you insist, you can pay me later; we can reveal who you are to the manager and eat for free. I never paid a check with less regret.

Another afternoon, Nelle asked me to read a letter from Alice. She complained that her sister wrote in such tiny script that no one could read the words. I replied that after four decades of grading six thousand students' exams, I could read or at least interpret any handwriting. But I did struggle to read Alice's tiny letters, especially her signature. Nelle finally rescued me by explaining that Alice signed all her family letters with the nickname, "Bear."

After a half year of grueling rehab, Nelle received news that changed her mood entirely. President George W. Bush was awarding her the Presidential Medal of Freedom at a White House ceremony on November 5, 2007. She told us that her main concern was the wheelchair: "I am not going to receive that medal sitting in a wheelchair!" I told her not to worry. The President would be surrounded by Marines who would gladly help her. "I am NOT sitting in the chair!" she repeated with typical Lee-family finality.

And she did not. She redoubled her physical therapy. After traveling by train to Washington with attorney Susan Doss, a tall Marine wrapped her hands around his arm and walked her to the podium. The President of the United States read the citation, then stepped toward her. He placed her left hand tightly around his right arm and her right hand just as tightly clenched on the top of his arm. She broke into an embarrassed smile for the ages as he presented her the nation's highest civilian award.

The long round trip to Washington convinced Nelle that she could manage a less restrictive and boring life than the past six months had afforded. She checked herself out of Lakeshore and reluctantly moved to Monroeville to begin a new life. In retrospect, Dartie and I concluded the move was a mistake, because the physical therapy at Lakeshore was more demanding and regular.

Three years later, when Barack Obama awarded Nelle the National Medal of the Arts, the nation's most prestigious award for writers, she gladly accepted but declined a return trip to the White House, complaining that it was too hard to repeat the train ride.

One of life's ironies is how people compartmentalize friendships. Some friends we know from childhood and never lose touch with. Other best friends fade from our consciousness when we leave for college, marry, move to a different state, change ideologies or political affiliation. New friendships begin in middle age or even later.

After Nelle died, we often thought that if we had known her earlier in our lives, we might not have liked her so well, nor she us. She had enjoyed exceptional health. She was opinionated (as am I) to the point of damned cantankerousness. Dartie was more malleable and kept her opinions mainly to herself. When an acquaintance of mine entreated Nelle to allow an acclaimed novelist an interview, she scribbled, "Hell no!" in turquoise ink and returned the missive to its sender.

We did not know Harper Lee in her self-reliant ascendancy. We knew her in her physical and mental decline and dependency, when her vision and hearing failed and her loneliness increased. By then she was a different person from the often abrupt and sometimes offensive woman we heard others describe.

While she was in Lakeshore Rehabilitation Hospital, we came to know her well enough to understand that she loved authentic humor (but not silly jokes), word play, and mutual insults. During her last weeks there, I began "trading twelves" with her—a pattern of good-natured mutual insults rooted in African American musical tradition. I had first heard of it from Albert Murray, a gifted black writer who was a native of Mobile, Alabama. He had met Ralph Ellison when they were students at Tuskegee Institute and talented members of the college band. Both later moved to Harlem where Ellison's novel, *Invisible Man*, rocked the literary world. Murray was a devotee of jazz and big band music; his biography of Duke Ellington and his memoir *South to a Very Old Place* employed jazz idiom and slang to explore black identity.

Part of that identity was trading twelves, which mirrors an

impromptu jazz session where musicians improvise twelve bars of music around the same musical idea. Their "dialogue" riffs back and forth, exchanging ideas and emotions. Similarly, when performed well, trading twelves is infused with competition but also with humor, warmth, skill, and smarts. In fact, it is most fun when friends engage in a contest to claim the clinching final twelve.

Dartie never liked games, thought the whole thing silly, and refused to participate. Nelle loved trading twelves as much as I did and was quite skilled right up to her death. I rationalized to Dartie that the exercise was harmless, therapeutic, and a sure antidote to Nelle's depression and melancholy. It also was fine mental exercise during her final years.

DURING AN OCTOBER 2014 visit, the duty nurse told us that our appearance was a waste of time because Nelle could not hear anything. Nonetheless, we visited, and I shouted to Nelle that I would be flying to Holland, Michigan, for a series of lectures at Hope College about the Lee sisters and *To Kill a Mockingbird*. There is a sad backstory. I asked students in two psychology classes to read a passage from *Mockingbird* before I arrived. The passage would constitute my introduction to a discussion of class relationships among whites in a small Deep South town during the Great Depression. The passage described Scout's invitation to a shoeless poor farm boy for dinner and an overnight stay. Scout's Aunt Alexandra scotched that idea because "that boy is not like you!" A month later, after I finished the last of my lectures at Hope College, a member of the audience told me that Alice Lee had died that day. The news was shattering. Despite her age of 103, it was hard for me to imagine Monroeville, or even Alabama, without her.

When we next visited and I told Nelle about the lectures, she did not remember details about the Scout/farm boy passage (my graduate students often remembered more about my books than I did, so I did not assume either of us was drifting into dementia). That is the day I launched our first session of trading twelves: "You really ought to read the novel, Nelle. It's quite good!" She was primed for the game. "Well, I should ask you for fifty dollars for helping you with your lecture." "No, Nelle, you owe me fifty dollars for selling forty copies of your book to the psychology students." After several more riffs, she looked straight at Dartie and asked: "How can you stand being married to a crazy man?" Before Dartie could answer, I interrupted: "Because she is as crazy as I am!" I thought I won that round of twelves. Dartie was not amused.

Nelle and Dartie seemed to have conspired on other occasions. Nelle began by describing one of her lifetime Monroeville friends with a by-now familiar caveat: "She was a wonderful woman married to a horror!" I steeled myself for yet another salacious story of sexual infidelity or spousal abuse in a Southern version of Peyton Place. Instead, we sat in silence until her perfectly timed twelve: "Just like you, Dartie!"

A year later Nelle was in a competitive mood when we arrived. She began the contest, and I warned her to be careful because she had asked me to present a eulogy for her when she died, which meant I would have the last word. She was much too clever to have me preempt death: "Suppose you go first?" "Well, in that eventuality I know you too well to let you into heaven," I replied. Having triumphed, I was not surprised when she launched a different riff. Looking at Dartie, she riffed, "You're smart! He's not."

Before I could think how to respond to so obvious a trap, she changed the subject by showing us a photograph she had received from an extremely muscular British working-class chap featuring a large mockingbird tattoo in her honor. I pounced on the opportunity to string together riffs about the kind of men who send women pictures of their tattoos.

She took public revenge on me during a performance of *King Lear* at the Alabama Shakespeare Festival. She had sponsored the production, only months before her death. Rumors of dementia had been circulating, compounded by her nearly complete deafness (to communicate with her, I had to shout inches from her right ear). Unable to hear the actors even when sitting in the wheelchair section a few yards from the stage, she loudly interrupted the first act numerous times asking what they were saying. We were in our season ticket seats some distance away and were still able to hear the racket. Worse yet, the combination of her questions followed by her recitation of lines she had memorized decades earlier from her favorite Shakespearean play were confusing even the professional cast. Anyone witnessing the tumult would have sworn the woman in the wheelchair section was as mad as King Lear. A friend mercifully wheeled her away to the patrons' lounge where Tonja Carter had arranged a fancy reception. As they filed into the lounge at intermission, I carefully plotted my revenge for her embarrassment of me in our last match of trading twelves. I walked directly to Nelle's wheelchair, where she was sitting alone, knelt beside her, and said loudly, "Nelle, you could be King Lear!" Silence descended quickly enough for me to realize that no one other than the two of us understood the great fun of trading insults. Everyone else was horrified. I need not have worried about my reputation. Before I could persuade my creaky knee to help me stand up, she shouted as loudly as I had: "And YOU could be my fool!" After seconds of silence, laughter exploded across the room.

A week later when we visited her in Monroeville, I had thought of another riff. Reminding her of my public defenestration at the Shakespeare Festival, I chided her: "Remember that in Shakespeare's plays the 'fool' is almost always smarter than the king." My riff elicited no shame from her, only a smirk. But I knew what she was thinking: "Nice try, buddy, but your riff was a week late, a dollar short, and seven day-delays are not allowed when trading twelves."

Her literary scholar-nephew, Ed Conner, sent me a poignant explanation of Nelle's preference for *King Lear* among the corpus of Shakespearean plays. It is the story of an old man's unjust treatment of his daughter, their alienation and reconciliation, and her rediscovery of his humanity, a plot not unlike that in *Go Set a Watchman*.

Chapter 12

Exile in Babylon

HAVING PROVEN TO HERSELF THAT SHE COULD LIVE BEYOND THE restrictive confines of Lakeshore, the question was "Where next?" Moving back to Manhattan at age eighty-one, partially paralyzed, would have been a complex challenge, despite the presence there of so many friends. Alice argued persuasively for Monroeville because of her own age, ninety-six, her enormous influence throughout southwest Alabama, her contacts with the medical community, and the simplicity for Nelle of living close to relatives and Alabama friends.

The Meadows Assisted Living, a simple facility with only sixteen rooms, a kitchen, and a commons area for meals and conversation, had a small room immediately available, with a larger one pending. In 2007, despite her preference for New York, Harper Lee returned to the town she had fled from fifty-eight years earlier. One of her New York City friends noted that the worst part of the stroke for Nelle was having to return to Monroeville.

Dartie and I visited a few weeks after she settled into The Meadows and were greeted by a highly agitated woman. We initially assumed this was collateral damage from her forced return to a place she did not want to be. It turned out to be a less worrisome crisis. Somehow she had misplaced a photograph that President and Mrs. George W. Bush had autographed for her when she received the Presidential Medal. She dispatched me to find it. I searched in obvious places such as closets, boxes, and dresser drawers. As she murmured, "How could I have lost it?" with escalating anxiety, I looked in coat pockets, through her clothes, papers, everywhere. Alas, having unfolded every piece of clothing, examined every nook and cranny of the room, even looking under the bed, I could not find the missing photograph.

I finally told her not to worry. I was flying to Washington the following week (which was true), so I would stop by the White House and explain that Harper Lee had lost her autographed photo of the first family and would like to have a signed replacement (which, of course, was not true). We had only recently begun trading twelves, so she was not certain when I was serious or just messing with her mind. She carefully studied my face before exploding into laughter. Before our next visit, she had moved into a two-room apartment where the photograph of her with the Bushes had somehow turned up and now graced the wall.

Her higher challenge was to adjust to a new regimen of rehabilitation. At Lakeshore, the staff had tried to please her by pretending she was just another patient when in fact she was a superstar. In the small Meadows facility, she might be a celebrity patient, but from the perspective of overworked staff, she really was just another long-term resident. They were kind and attentive but had lots of others to care for.

Her dining table mates until their deaths were the only two male residents. The three seemed to get along as well as partially deaf people could. Most of the female residents gave Nelle a wide berth, whether from dislike, jealousy at her frequent visitors from afar, or because the men dined with her, we never determined.

The staff was fabulous. After the initial uproar and their adjustment to Nelle's irascibility, they were thoroughly professional. We did not envy them taking care of a woman who was world-famous, nearly blind and deaf, and highly opinionated.

In time she lapsed into the stoicism characteristic of the Lee family. One of my favorite devotional writers, Sarah Breathitt, observed that "in time we become the custodian of our own contentment." That heroic description certainly characterized the last decade of Nelle's life. "The Usual Suspects" visited as frequently as they could. Nelle, of course, continued to preside as "prime suspect." The cabal sometimes arrived in their blue shirts with attached pins, and Nelle took special delight in frequent reminders in my presence that the clique admitted no males. I told her my feelings were hurt when my friend Gorman Houston, an associate justice of the Alabama Supreme Court, claimed to be an honorary member. She laughed derisively but finally conferred that inferior rank on me as well. She emphasized that the secret society would hold no meetings or engage in any projects. There were two celebratory events. The first was in May 2008 in Montgomery when Nelle was presented honorary membership in the Alabama Bar Association. When Gorman asked her for a list of guests to invite, her cryptic reply was, "Round up the usual suspects." The second was our favorite gathering, a boisterous party in Monroeville in 2015 at Tonja Carter's restaurant to celebrate publication of *Go Set a Watchman*. That event brought friends from London, New York City, and many places.

SUCH JOYOUS BUT INFREQUENT shenanigans had a short shelf life amid the routine boredom of The Meadows. And when excitement occurred, it was often of the bad variety. The most egregious incident was the invasion by the British reporter who barged into her room, then wrote an unflattering article about a handicapped and grouchy old woman. Following that episode, visitors were screened more carefully.

Nelle's closest friends were scattered and busy with their own lives, so her socialization and recreation consisted of whatever The Meadows' staff provided. Mostly she remained alone in her room, reading books on her magnification machine, ate, slept, and was bored. Alice and Tonja visited regularly and "The Usual Suspects" as often as possible. Sometimes Dartie and I wondered if including us in her small circle had more to do with her loneliness and our availability than anything else. Surviving in assisted living is largely a matter of attitude and diversion.

For years Nelle's diversion had been gambling. There were many layers to Alice Lee's Christianity. She was the most disciplined person we knew, the most morally upright, and the most trusting of others, often to her detriment. Among her best attributes was her non-judgmental Christianity, especially toward her baby sister. Although Alice never condemned Nelle's lifestyle, neither did she commend it. As decades passed and Nelle's declining health required alterations such as stopping smoking and tempering her consumption of alcohol, Alice grew increasingly anxious. Following Nelle's stroke, rehab, and reluctant consent to live at The Meadows, Alice made a concession of her own: She regularly gave Nelle $250 to $450 to gamble at the Creek Indian casino in Atmore, a small town similar to and some twenty miles south of Monroeville. Two of "The Usual Suspects" and Tom Butts, a former Methodist pastor, usually transported her, and Tonja hired drivers on other occasions. Alice told us that she saw no harm in it, that Nelle enjoyed the outing whatever the outcome, could certainly afford to lose, and was "making a handsome contribution to the Creek Indians." Although Nelle oftentimes won, according to several of the "The Usual Suspects," she never admitted that to us. (Legalized gambling was and is highly controversial in Alabama, but federally recognized Indian tribes, like Alabama's Creeks, can operate casinos on their reservations. They do, and the expansive operations are lucrative.)

On Nelle's birthday in 2011, Alice treated her to a gambling spree with extra money. We arrived while she was still at the casino. When she returned, I asked if she had won. She began by insisting that she had won a lot, initially. Then her lamentation began: "I lost my shirt, my britches, and my shoes. Alice is going to kill me!" It is useful here to note that before Alice grew too infirm to do so, she handled Nelle's finances and provided to Nelle whatever money she needed when she needed or wanted it. Following Alice's move to assisted living, her law partner, Tonja Carter, continued to manage Nelle's finances.

Although neither Dartie nor I gambled, we volunteered to drive her to Atmore during our monthly trips. Tonja told us to stop by the office for cash. She explained that it would not require much of our time because Nelle usually lost every dollar on the electronic poker machines. I inquired what we should do while she gambled: Remain with her? Sit and read? "Oh no," she replied. "Nelle likes to gamble alone, although you might check on her occasionally." Tonja said the casino's restaurant was fine, and by the time we finished a meal, Nelle would have lost her money.

I assured her that we would dole out the cash as needed. Tonya responded that she trusted us because we were "like family."

Two incidents ended Nelle's gambling outings. One of her local drivers allegedly stole some of her money, thinking, I suppose, that she would not know what happened. Nelle also fell once while shifting from her wheelchair into a car. A month later when we called, Tonja said Nelle had lost interest in gambling. We heard later that someone had accosted her on a slack day in the casino and had terrified her into giving him her money. Whether from fear of falling or of other people, she never mentioned gambling again. We did not consider this so much a triumph for our negative view of gambling as a sadness that she had lost the joy of living her way rather than ours.

A DISPUTE WITH SAMUEL "Sam" Pinkus delivered the second and more personal blow to her life in confinement. Nelle preferred not to be bothered by financial details of her fame, leaving that to her agent, and Alice, her tax expert.

With us, Nelle's first references to Pinkus were reverential. She said that as older partners died in her second literary agency, McIntosh & Otis, Pinkus "inherited" her through the influence of his wife, Elizabeth, the daughter of Eugene Winick, the agency's eventual president. As years passed, Nelle grew fond of Elizabeth and her two sons. Sam Pinkus shielded Nelle from publicity and financial details and became her traveling companion on train trips. He also aggressively negotiated royalty contracts with her publisher. From our external observations, he was treated like a member of the family, even attending birthday parties.

In the early days of their friendship, I asked about him. "He is the quintessential New York literary agent," she answered. "He's Jewish. A little owl-like man. Smart and knowledgeable. He is wonderful." When Alice told us that Nelle's contract with Harper-Collins was expiring, I asked if Pinkus was going to renew the contract.* She surprised us by responding that the publisher had offered fifteen million dollars for rights to continue publishing *To Kill a Mockingbird*, but Pinkus did not think it enough. Three years later when we visited Alice and Nelle, they were sharply critical of Pinkus concerning a copyright dispute about *Mockingbird*. On our trip home that evening, we ruminated again about our writer friend Mary Ward Brown's aphorism, "This fame stuff will kill you."

Food was a tranquilizing comfort amidst such controversies. Her appetite varied from vigorous to voracious. Although plump from lack of exercise and too many sweets, she was never obese. After her two male table mates died, a childhood neighbor began sitting with her at meals at The Meadows. One day when we joined them for conversation, the woman told us about having made hand-churned ice cream for Nelle once when she was on a visit home. She knew this was a delicacy not common in New York, and nearly everyone in the South had a favorite flavor and recipe. She brought two containers, one for Nelle, the other for Alice. Nelle ate her portion with gusto, then opened Alice's and began eating it, chuckling: "Alice is still at the office; she will never know."

---

*   *To Kill a Mockingbird* was published in 1960 by J. B. Lippincott & Co., which merged in 1978 with Harper & Row, which was acquired by Murdoch's News Corporation in 1987 and eventually merged with another imprint, becoming HarperCollins, which published *Go Set a Watchman* in 2015.

One Christmas as we returned from a vacation on the Alabama gulf coast, we stopped at our favorite restaurant which was famous for seafood and Key lime pie. When we arrived, the parking lot was empty and I was about to drive away when a man came out the door. I asked a dumb question given the circumstances: "Are you closed?" "Yes," he replied, "we are closed for Christmas." I told him I was disappointed because the restaurant's Key lime pie was my favorite, and I wanted to take a pie to a writer friend, Harper Lee. I know that was name-dropping, but at least it was true. He seemed momentarily stunned before replying: "THE Harper Lee?" "Yes, she is a friend of ours." He asked me to wait a moment, unlocked the door and emerged a few minutes later with a pie. When I tried to pay, he smiled and said: "Tell her it is a Christmas gift from the Original Oyster House." Whether he was manager or owner, even his name, we never knew, but I thought of him that day as one of the Magi on the way to Bethlehem with gifts.

A couple of hours later, as we walked through the commons area of The Meadows with our beautiful pie in a clear plastic container, every resident and staff member seemed laser-focused on the pie. We resolved to buy three pies the next year so that all at The Meadows could have a slice. That became part of the Flynt family Christmas ritual until Nelle died. At Nelle's room, I cut a piece of pie and offered her a bite. She tasted the tart sweetness and asked, "What is the name of that pie?" in a tone of voice that barely masked displeasure. Given the trouble we had gone to, I replied a bit despondently, "Key lime." "No," she shouted, "Its name is More! More!"

Another culinary revelation was the day we brought her a bag of Ghirardelli Dark Chocolate Raspberry Squares. We already knew she loved chocolate but learned that day that raspberry was her favorite fruit. The single squares were enclosed in tight wrapping that was hard to open, so I tore the edge of one, uncovering half the candy. Normally the squares are a delicate two- or three-bite treat to be savored. But as her mouth rapidly approached my finger, I realized she was aiming for the entire square. I barely released it in time to save my thumb and finger. I joked that I finally understood her childhood obsession with a book about cannibals. She laughed uproariously. Henceforth, she followed each piece of candy by chanting, "More! More!" We finally happened on the origin of that line as "More. That's right! I want more" in the 1948 Humphrey Bogart movie, *Key Largo*.

During Nelle's first years in assisted living, we sometimes took her and Alice to David's Catfish Restaurant, a Monroeville favorite for fried catfish, one of the South's favorite sources of cholesterol. Nelle would fill her plate with fried fish and hush puppies (a small fried ball of cornmeal dough) and wash them down with sweet iced tea. Alice would munch delicately on oysters or shrimp and drink water. Food at The Meadows itself was as healthy as Southern country cooking usually is, which means not very. Nelle's favorites were fried chicken or meat loaf, and macaroni and cheese, followed by fruit cobbler. As for homemade sweets, Nelle need not have worried. Dartie cooked cakes, pies, and fudge brownies for her, and in season brought fresh peaches and blueberries from nearby farms.

DURING HER YEARS AT The Meadows, Nelle's moods vacillated between depression, melancholy, loneliness, and spirited and witty conversations with friends and visitors. When she was depressed, we countered with our entire repertoire of stories about her namesake in our family. When our son David and Kelly, his wife, moved to Seattle, I assumed Dartie's Parkinson's Disease would make visits infrequent or impossible. That assumption ignored her courage, determination, and the birth of grandson Dallas and the first female Flynt in three generations of our immediate family. Kelly was a prodigious reader of history and fiction, so their choice of "Harper" as a given name was no surprise. In fact, since the publication of *Mockingbird*, "Harper" has continuously been among our nation's top ten female given names, most of them, I surmised, bestowed on daughters of feminist women such as my daughter-in-law. When we shared that information with Nelle, she was delighted.

Meeting the little dynamo was a different matter. The two Harpers first laid eyes on each other in the magnificent lobby of the Alabama Department of Archives and History in Montgomery where Nelle was receiving yet another honor. Our children flew home from Seattle with their two-year-old daughter for the event. Nelle was no great fan of children of any age, but especially not a squiggly two-year-old. The photograph of the event shows me holding Harper Flynt for an introduction while Harper Lee—forcing a smile—moves in the opposite direction lest the small creature reach out for her. Meanwhile, Little Harper shows no interest whatever in writers famous or obscure. Some months passed before Kelly wrote us that Little Harper had received a beautiful, miniature tea set from a fine boutique in New York City sent by Big Harper.

More months passed before we flew to Seattle to care for our grandchildren while their parents celebrated their tenth anniversary in Italy. Although Dartie tried to teach Harper manners by hosting a proper and dignified tea party using her new tea set, augmented by spiffy hats and frilly dresses, Harper remained a typical strong-willed three-year-old hellion, probably lots like her namesake at a similar age. The next morning I took her to the nearest children's park as penance for shutting her away crying after a temper tantrum the night before. The only people present were a young woman and her daughter about Harper's age. As always in such situations, I had brought a book to read. The young woman had her own book (after all this was suburban Seattle). We sat at opposite ends of a long bench reading our books in mutual silence as the children played together. Suddenly, the woman shouted, "Harper! Stop that right now!" I was shocked. How dare she shout at my granddaughter! That was my prerogative. But when I transferred my focus from her to the object of her anger, I realized she was correcting her daughter, not my granddaughter.

Almost reflexively I asked, "Is your daughter named Harper?" "Yes," was her abrupt one-word answer. Before I could suppress the urge, I asked how she chose that name, thinking the answer might enrich my lectures about the worldwide influence of Alabama's remarkable literary culture and perhaps begin a conversation to pass the time while the children played. "It's the name of my favorite author," she replied while lowering her eyes back to the privacy of her book. The ensuing silence and body language made it clear she did not talk to aging male strangers in parks.

Being by nature a garrulous extrovert, I briefly considered interrupting her again: "I know this is hard for you to believe, but I live in Alabama, my granddaughter is named Harper, and Harper Lee is one of my dearest friends." As I considered further the differences in our ages, the circumstances of our meeting, the absence of any other people, and the possible consequences of her misinterpreting entirely what was happening, I could hardly contain my laughter. I speculated about the speed with which she would either depart or dial 911. She would either consider what I said the worst, most pathetic "pick-up" line she had ever heard, or, even worse, report a dirty old man accosting her in a public park.

I did not speak another word. She soon gathered her daughter and departed. We followed soon after. I pondered how whimsical life can be. Had she seemed open and friend to aging strangers with Southern accents, I could have spent an hour or so as the children played telling her about her favorite author. No doubt we would have marveled at the mathematical chances of two strangers meeting in a park with only four people, including two children named Harper, both named for the same Alabama author. She would have been enthralled as I spun the story that would become this book.

I knew Harper Lee would love the story because the possible outcome could have been a long distance telephone call from the Lake Forest Park, Washington, jail for her verification of my identity and our relationship, which she might or might not have given depending on the outcome of our last session trading twelves.

When we told Nelle the story on our next visit, we had never seen her laugh so much. From that time until her death, that was the best tonic for her bouts of melancholia. On the rare occasions when that story failed to lift her spirit, I had an alternative. One afternoon when David and his family were visiting my mother, I noticed the U.S. Mail truck approaching on my mother's long driveway. I asked Harper, then four, if she wanted to walk with me to the mailbox. The female letter carrier met us and handed the mail to Little Harper. As the woman drove away, I told Little Harper, "Maybe you will be a mail-lady when you grow up." She was quiet for a moment, then replied unhappily: "I'm no lady! I'm Harper Swann Flynt!" Every time I told Big Harper that story, she supplied the same postscript: "You tell Harper that I'm no lady either!"

As our Harper grew older, she demonstrated theatrical skills commensurate with her ambition to someday be on Broadway. She became adept in Irish step dance, began to compose and sing her own music, won ever more challenging roles in Seattle area community theater productions, and charted a course toward universities with musical theater programs. Big Harper's interest in her namesake grew parallel to Little Harper's preoccupation with acting.

WHEN OUR GRANDDAUGHTER WAS ten, we spent a week together at the beach. On our return to Auburn, we stopped in Monroeville to allow the two Harpers a last chat before their ways parted. Our grandchildren's favorite memory from that day was what by then had become a ritual: a Key lime pie brought from the Original Oyster House, the first bite fed to Nelle, her smirky grimace and shout, "What's the name of that pie?" My reply, "Key lime." Her correction: "No! It's MORE! MORE!" We were all laughing before the pie was consumed.

Because of a controversy about a new book written about her which claimed to be written with her consent, I had brought a column by a good friend, John Archibald, winner of a Pulitzer Prize for commentary. He had projected Harper Lee into various characters from her novel, concluding correctly that she identified with Boo Radley, the secretive and private person who just wanted to be left alone. He movingly defended her right to privacy, arguing that all who claimed to love her should grant her that entirely reasonable request. When I finished reading the column to Nelle, she was deeply moved but said nothing. I noticed that David had brought his camera. But he was so affected by Archibald's column that he departed without photographs of that last meeting of the two Harpers, allowing it to remain in our memories where the image will never fade. Our grandchildren Harper and Dallas left The Meadows smitten by the woman we now called "the great one" or "Big Harper," but also aware that fame often contains its own heartbreak.

Back in Seattle, Dallas's English teacher assigned *To Kill a Mockingbird*. When Dallas interrupted his teacher's introduction of the author to describe Harper Lee to his classmates, the teacher reacted with disbelief; Dallas had to bring photos of Big Harper and Little Harper together years earlier at the award ceremony at the Alabama state archives.

A week after Christmas that year, Nelle greeted us wearing her seasonal "Roll Tide" sweatshirt. I had prepared my rejoinder in anticipation of such humiliation following Auburn's football loss once again to the Crimson Tide. During the holidays, our son David had invited Little Harper to sing the national anthem. She complied with her rendition of the Auburn University fight song: "War Eagle, fly down the field, ever to conquer, never to yield. . . ." Her older brother chided her for singing about Auburn rather than the national anthem. Pausing momentarily to consider his reprimand, she continued with the Auburn fight song. A nurse who had chosen that moment to check on Nelle heard the gale of laughter as she opened the door. Later she told us that she had not heard Nelle laugh like that since Alice's death.

We informed Nelle that day that her namesake had won her first "starring" role in Seattle community theater, for which she would be paid her first "professional earnings." I had carefully planned my next line: "Were you paid for your first writing before age ten?" "No, of course not," she grumbled.

Dartie changed the subject by giving Nelle a beautifully sculpted and polished heart-shaped piece of marble from the famous quarries in Sylacauga, Alabama, the only place in the world outside Carrera, Italy, with exquisite white marble. Our Alabama sculptor friend and Guggenheim Fellow, Craigger Brown, had made two marble hearts as Christmas presents for Dartie and Nelle. (He would later sculpt a magnificent mockingbird rising from azalea bushes for us.) As Nelle ran her hand back and forth over the exquisitely polished marble, she murmured, "Why would someone I do not know give me something so beautiful?" Dartie answered, "Because you are famous all over the world, Nelle!" All the humor of Little Harper's fight song melted away as she told us once again, "No one knows me." Then fixing her eyes on Dartie's cane, she muttered, "I hope you don't have to stay in a wheelchair." The drive home that afternoon seemed longer than usual, each of us lost in our own thoughts.

Despite Nelle's long confinement, she continued her literary life even in The Meadows. As her vision worsened, her painstakingly arduous reading gravitated from fiction to history to theology. Near the end of her life, a volume of love letters exchanged between Robert E. Lee and his wife competed with the anthology of C. S. Lewis's writings for her attention.

As for fiction, I sometimes read to her novels that were sufficiently clever, humorous, and well-written to hold her attention. On her eighty-fourth birthday, I brought *Major Pettigrew's Last Stand*, the delightful first novel by British writer Helen Simonson, who grew up in a small village in East Sussex but was then living in Brooklyn. The plot followed the romance of a retired, widowed British Army officer living in Sussex after years of service in India, and a hardworking Pakistani convenience store owner and widow. Predictably, the main impediment to their marriage was their supercilious and bigoted children. As I read the first chapter aloud, Nelle was quiet, intensely interested, and laughed in all the right places. I was astounded at her concentration.

Nelle's refusal to use her hearing aid or allergy medicine limited my reading to one chapter a visit because my voice would become hoarse. Dartie coached me in how to "read" the chapters as if they were oral interpretations of literature—the kind of events she had often narrated in our church's special worship services. "Change your voice when the characters change," she admonished. "Interject humor, pathos, embarrassment, anger, the sort of things a retired British army officer would experience when courting an East Asian immigrant to the embarrassment of both sets of children." I vigorously demurred one day, shouting in a loud voice to Nelle that Dartie was the thespian in the family, not me. I was only an historian. That day our exaggerated argument vied with Simonson's novel in entertainment value, so far as Nelle was concerned.

Usually we could distract her foul temper but not always.

During a birthday visit in April 2009 when she was talkative, spry, and happy, Supreme Court Justice Gorman Houston called. Dartie was nearest the phone, so Nelle asked her to answer. Gorman did not recognize Dartie's voice and, fearing he had rung the wrong number, asked who she was. When she replied, he asked, "Are you Wayne Flynt's wife?" Although Dartie sometimes threatened to answer that question with "No, the last name is just a coincidence," in this instance she said yes, and he asked to speak to me. We chatted about our mutual friend Louise Conner and Alabama politics for a while, until I noticed that Nelle was unhappy at our extended conversation. I passed the phone to her, and she began their chat with a decidedly angry comment: "Hello, Gorman! Anytime you want to talk with Wayne Flynt, just call me and I will get him for you!"

The following year, on a miserably hot Alabama day when the temperature rose to a hundred degrees, we were distressed to hear a wheeze in Nelle's lung. She also had a persistent cough. We mentioned taking her to lunch at Sweet Tooth Bakery and Deli, the excellent cafe on the town square. The oppressive heat, her wheezing, and complaints about shoulder pain (we learned later that she had fallen and torn her rotator cuff) discouraged us, but she insisted on going anyway. As I pushed her wheelchair to our car, every bump elicited a "Rats" from her. We had even more trouble getting her into the car. Her frustration mounted as she tried various angles unsuccessfully. "Rats" turned to "Damn!" Without an ounce of self-pity but with rising anger and frustration, she would have lost the struggle except for Dartie's humor and perceptive engineering skills. She instructed Nelle to turn around with her back to the open door and clasp the door frame with her good hand. Then she told me to move the wheelchair away. Her last instruction to Nelle was "lower your head, point your butt at the seat, let go of the door frame, and fall." Miraculously, it worked perfectly. Nelle fell backwards, cleared the car roof by inches, steadied herself on the seat, and laughed as if she had won the pole vaulting medal at the Olympics. We congratulated her for her conquest of gravity.

At the cafe, she instructed me to fill her plate with chicken pot pie, turnip greens, macaroni and cheese, and cornbread, and to bring a glass of iced tea. The meal became a side bar to Dartie's hysterical description of Nelle's "lift-off" from the parking lot as if she were on an Apollo mission bound for the moon. For anyone who had witnessed it, the meal would have been an anti-climax.

Our last meal together at Sweet Tooth was just as memorable for a different reason. Venturing out of The Meadows to eat in a town where everyone recognized Harper Lee had more risks than just falling. Only once or twice had someone who recognized her stopped at the table to speak to her. Monroeville people called such occasions a "sighting" they could discuss with friends and relatives but not interrupt. Dartie and I considered the locals' restraint in such social situations among the town's finest qualities. At this midday, surrounded by a restaurant full of local folks who recognized Nelle immediately, I carried her tray to our table while conversations modulated to a whisper, then nearly ended altogether. I was facing the door and noticed a woman who had finished her meal and was heading out the door when she executed a 180 turn and headed for our table. Nelle's back was to the woman, but I could tell from the straight-line escalating speed that the woman was not to be stopped.

As I anticipated, the excited lady barely made it to our table before telling Nelle's back: "Miss Lee, my mother was a student with you at Monroe County High School!" Given the silence that had descended on the room, she could have been announcing this with a bullhorn. Deaf as a stump that day, Nelle was disoriented by the sound, couldn't see the woman, and asked loudly, "What did she say?" I repeated the statement loudly enough for her and half of Monroeville to hear. Nelle turned partially in her direction, flashed a smile, and asked: "What was your mother's name, honey?" The woman said her mother's name, which I loudly repeated to Nelle. Nelle radiated a smile that could only be described as beatific and replied, "Your mother was the sweetest thing!" The woman said nothing else but virtually levitated across the room and out the door, as Nelle turned to us and shouted, "Who the hell was that?" Perhaps she remembered more of that event than I realized, because that was the last time she would join us for lunch outside The Meadows.

As EARLY AS 2011, Alice shared with us concerns about Nelle's health, especially her memory. Alice had a better baseline from which to judge Nelle's rapier wit and sisterly banter. Nelle had always preferred books, Broadway productions, and convivial intellectual company to frivolous friends. So by Alice's standards (or even by our own in our seventies), a "decline" from the baseline that others knew left plenty of smarts, as Nelle's humor and clever mastery of trading twelves demonstrated. Alice also attributed some of Nelle's cognitive problems to her obstinate refusal to wear her hearing aids or use prescribed ear drops for her allergies.

During a 2014 controversy concerning a book about Harper Lee, the author claimed that Nelle had agreed to be interviewed for publication. The attorney in Alice attributed that claim to Nelle's deafness and embarrassment in not understanding questions. That was particularly true when trying to understand softer women's voices. When Dartie and I visited, I sometimes felt like a translator, repeating Dartie's comments to Nelle and hers to Dartie. My habit was to position myself ten to twelve inches from Nelle's right ear and shout. I also noticed that when asked to sign anything, Nelle usually said "sure," placed the book or document on her magnification machine without even reading what it was, and signed. Partly that was because no one she did not already know was allowed into her room at The Meadows.

The contrasting health of the two sisters was remarkable. Alice used her hearing aid during our visits and was keen intellectually when she entered assisted living at age one hundred and two. She greeted us at our first visit after her move by exclaiming that she had read about a fundraiser for Birmingham Community Ministries, a Methodist charity, where I had performed with a former student who was also a well-known songwriter, musician, and vocalist. I had read passages from Southern literature, including *Mockingbird*, about which my student had composed songs. I told Alice that Dartie was a fine coach on such occasions, when she could have performed far better than I did.

We left Alice's facility and drove to The Meadows where Tonja Carter was having Nelle sign legal documents. Nelle was wearing her hearing aid and heard us plainly. She was dressed in her "Roll Tide" sweater and, with only a little provocation from me, burst into her aggravating 1940s chant about the University of Alabama on the Black Warrior River. A stranger would never have known that several months earlier she seemed lost in a fog.

On our next visit she tormented me again with the chant. Although she had a cold, her mind was clear and sharp. She recounted stories she had written for the *Rammer Jammer* while a student at the university, and provocative articles she had authored for the *Crimson-White* student newspaper.

Although physicians can determine with a high degree of accuracy whether a person has it based on medical history, laboratory tests, and changes in thinking processes and behaviors, dementia is a complicated disease that covers a wide range of memory loss. Because dementia occurs in half of Parkinson's patients, all three of Dartie's neurologists tracked her memory. Her first doctor in Birmingham diagnosed early stage dementia fifteen years before her death, when she was unable to remember all five words the doctor listed. When her new Auburn neurologist used the same test, I noticed that, after the conversation, he failed to ask her to repeat the words, instead asking his receptionist to schedule a follow-up examination, then returning to his office, and shutting the door. I knocked and reminded him that he had forgotten to ask Dartie to repeat the five words. He laughed and said that was not a definitive test, and if it were, he might be suffering from the same disease. After that doctor retired, Dartie's third neurologist tracked her mental health to her death without significant symptoms of dementia despite twenty-one years of Parkinson's and a family history of dementia.

My point is not to dispute any medical diagnosis that Nelle might have had about memory problems or even dementia. My point is that the progress of dementia varies from person to person, and Nelle was functionally capable of both memory and cognitive function such as accurately repeating stories and anecdotes as late as the week before her death. Most rumors of her dementia were perpetuated and spread by people who were never with her, had no knowledge of her medical history, and had no access to laboratory tests. Her isolation from public scrutiny and contact was not part of a conspiracy. It was a lifelong pattern resulting from her obsession for privacy. Hearing and vision problems late in her life only accelerated the pattern. To be clear, I will describe both occasionally troubling memory lapses we encountered during our visits with Nelle as well as her remarkable capacity to remember details of her life until the week it ended.

On her eighty-eighth birthday in April 2014, her nurse told us that Nelle was refusing to take ear drops or wear her hearing aid. When she hugged Dartie that day, I noticed she held on longer and tighter. Then as usual, she turned her cheek toward me for a perfunctory kiss. We brought her the first peaches of the year and read a birthday card featuring Charles Schultz's "Peanuts" cartoon characters, notably the aggressive, opinionated, and ill-tempered Lucy. I told her that she was sufficiently old and opinionated to have been Schultz's model for Lucy. The card read, "Happy Birthday to the one who keeps me sane." She immediately understood the irony of such a card involving three people our ages and exploded into laughter, followed by the comment, "I'm about as sane as the devil in hell," which caught us by surprise. Then all of us joined in the hilarity.

Despite Nelle's health problems, that was one of our best visits. She congratulated me on winning the Eugene Garcia Literary Scholar Award, and I joked that I was a writer posing as a historian and she was a historian trying to escape the confines of fiction. She heard every word, mused over them for a moment, then moved on to other subjects.

We gave her a bracelet of bright-colored rubber bands for her birthday made by Little Harper. As I placed it on Nelle's wrist, I explained that I had contemplated buying her a diamond and platinum bracelet but knew she objected to wearing jewelry. To our surprise, she wore the rubber-band bracelet the rest of the afternoon.

On a visit six months later, her hearing was as bad as before. When Dartie asked how she was doing, she delivered a variation of her stock response, "I'm doing tolerable, but I'm fine now that you are here." Dartie had brought her a homemade lemon icebox pie, and she wanted me to feed it to her.

Our ensuing conversation about C. S. Lewis was anything but superficial. Unfortunately, in the absence of personal contact with Harper Lee, people did what they often do, propagate salacious gossip. Southern small towns may not have a monopoly on such conversations, but rumors of dementia had become linked to collateral conspiracies about Nelle's attorney's manipulation of her finances. Yet that day she lucidly discussed the entire corpus of Lewis's books, even occasionally correcting me on sequence of publication. When our conversation shifted to Horton Foote, she was no less precise: "A great gentleman from a town like mine, and so kind."

Whatever we might have told the world about Nelle's sanity seemed publicly contradicted by her conduct at Alice's memorial service. Dartie and I saw a distraught Harper Lee being wheeled into Monroeville Methodist Church by her nephew Ed Conner, just before the service began. We sat near the back because the sanctuary was packed by church members and other admirers from across the state. The service had obviously been pre-planned by Alice: simple, elegant, and traditional. Martin Luther's hymn "A Mighty Fortress Is Our God" roared from the organ, followed by the hymn "The Church's One Foundation Is Jesus Christ Her Lord." The music and Scripture spanned centuries from biblical times to the Reformation to John and Charles Wesley, founders of Methodism. Hank Conner's granddaughter played "Amazing Grace," as she had years earlier for Louise's service in Eufaula. One of the many female Methodist ministers Alice had mentored preached an elegant eulogy. The front of the program contained the Wesleyan version of the Great Commission: "Do all the good you can, by all the means you can, in all the ways you can, in all the places you can, at all the times you can, to all the people you can, as long as you can." The creed summarized Alice Lee's life. The words are also inscribed on the bas relief on the wall of the education building which Nelle donated.

Emotions were as restrained as one would expect given Alice's long life and belief in immortality. Nelle sat with the family far from us. We began to hear what sounded like a moan from that area. It became louder and louder, and we could see family members trying to quieten her. Suddenly the rumors of dementia flooded over us. After the service, Lee relatives told us that Nelle could not hear anything and was loudly asking what the preacher was saying about Alice.

Whatever inaccurate accounts of her conduct spread around Monroeville after the service, her depression was real enough. When we visited a month later, a nurse warned us that she had grieved since the funeral: "She is alone now, no one left," she whispered.

I had a hunch I knew the antidote at least for that afternoon. I began with the story of the first day the two Harpers met at the

State Archives and ended with the two Harpers playing in the Seattle park. The gloom lifted at least for that day, and by the time we departed for home she was again laughing at the irony and confusion of life. I left a message on her magnifier: "God meant you to be a social historian and me to write a novel that won the Pulitzer Prize. God just switched us at birth."

Shortly before Nelle's eighty-ninth birthday, we took her a short article from the London-based *Economist* magazine mentioning her newly published novel *Go Set a Watchman*. She read the article on her magnifier, then asked if the accompanying photograph was of Alice.

"No, it's you, Nelle," I replied.

She studied the face more carefully, then muttered, "Look at all the gray hair."

"That's because you are eighty-nine years old, Nelle. You get gray hair during eighty-nine years!"

She laughed and told me, "You are a bad boy, Wayne. I started to say you were just a boy with gray hair but then I remembered to add the 'bad' part."

Dartie changed the subject abruptly, asking if she preferred to be called Nelle, Harper, or Doty.

"Doty," she replied, "because that is what the family calls me."

We never felt comfortable using that intimate family name. But it was a master stroke to change the conversation to a more pleasant subject than gray hair, aging, and her deceased sister before we departed for Auburn.

Chapter 13

Watchman: The Final Mystery

I OFTEN TOLD STUDENTS IN MY HISTORY CLASSES NOT TO WORRY overly much about dates. Chronology is important and involves a certain embarrassment potential if one confuses the American Civil War between 1861 and 1865 with the nation's more recent unpleasantness between 2016 and 2020. The meaning of events—how and why they transpired and in what sequence—is much more important.

In that historical context, it is important to understand that during 1957 Nelle submitted to her agent short stories with various names and a completed novel tentatively entitled "The Long Goodbye"—goodbye to Macomb/Monroeville and to her mother and brother (who died within six months of each other). These were fragments of what would become *Go Set a Watchman*. She wrote the stories in her late twenties when idealism often swells inversely to the sins and compromises of one's parents. In the case of a young Alabama woman already at war with many conventional traditions, institutions, and patterns of her Methodist church and college, of her sorority and socially elite students at the University of Alabama, Nelle Harper Lee was well on her way to a new identity in a very large and anonymous city.

Then there was her emerging racial consciousness. During her first decade and a half in New York, black teenager Emmett Till was murdered in Mississippi, President Dwight Eisenhower dispatched the 101st Airborne Division to Little Rock, Arkansas, to enforce racial integration of Central High School; Rosa Parks was arrested, triggering the Montgomery Bus Boycott; a desegregation campaign began in Birmingham; there were numerous incidents of resurgent racial violence; the South led the nation in lynchings of black men; and the Alabama legislature voted 98–1 to close the state's public schools rather than integrate them. That was the historical context that produced Harper Lee's first novel manuscript.

But rage is rarely the midwife of great literature. Nor is it necessarily rooted in the reality of what is, compared to the dream of what can be. Even Southern white parents with some moral compass urged their children to remain silent while in the eye of a racial storm. To speak against the day between 1950 and 1965 was to risk social ostracism, economic boycott, broken friendships, divided families, and possible violence.

Go Set a Watchman was written decades before the horrific slaughter of African Americans at Mother Emanuel AME Church in Charleston, South Carolina, by a self-avowed "Southern nationalist" and police killings of unarmed black men in states around the nation. However, similar outrages in the mid twentieth century were the context in which Nelle's first novel was written.

Like most places in America, Monroeville had its own unique history of racism. A Monroeville friend and local historian described some of it to me. Although many residents, including the Lee family, traveled to Mobile to shop at a Jewish-owned department store, the town also had a mercantile establishment owned by Meyer Katz, a Jew who had fled Russia to escape conscription into the army. He and his five sons lived quietly in Monroeville without meddling in local affairs, although Katz claimed to be able to identify hooded Ku Klux Klansmen who marched through town in the 1930s by the shoes he had sold them.

My friend worked tirelessly locating and preserving artifacts for Monroeville's courthouse museum. After becoming curious about an abandoned log cabin on the outskirts of town, he stopped one day to inspect it. Underneath a pile of trash, he found a KKK sign from the 1920s, which he rescued for the museum collection (though not for public display; no point in dredging up times best forgotten).

To Kill a Mockingbird was set during the Great Depression when despair and marginalization were biracial, where blacks "knew their place" and mainly remained in it. Their enforced submission permitted conservative, law-and-order, institutionally religious white elites to defend blacks from lynch mobs when whites chose to do so. By the 1950s, black patience had diminished, black challenges to racist institutions had increased, and white terrorism was more common.

Go Set a Watchman begins with Jean Louise Finch's long train ride home, a brief reunion with her family and fiancé, and a Sunday worship service at the Maycomb Methodist Church. The pastor's biblical text came from Isaiah 21: 2–7, King James translation, of course:

> A grievous vision is declared unto me; the treacherous dealer dealeth treacherously.... Therefore are my loins filled with pain.... My heart panted, fearfulness affrighted me: the night of

my pleasure hath he turned into fear unto me. Prepare the table, watch in the watchtower, eat, drink: arise ye princes, and anoint the shield. For thus hath the Lord said unto me, Go, set a watchman, let him declare what he seeth. And he saw a chariot with a couple of horsemen. . . . And he cried . . . Babylon is fallen . . . and all the graven images of her gods he hath broken into the ground. . . . The watchman said, The morning cometh, and also the night. . . . Within a year . . . all the glory of Kedar shall fail. . . .

The Hebrew nation would be ravaged by Assyrian invasion. Afterwards, would the "New Jerusalem" reinstate cultic rituals or Messianic social justice? Theologians refer to such passages as apocalyptic, meaning a prophetic revelation of coming events. Such language and prophecy were common in black as well as white evangelical churches in the twentieth century. The prophecy could not have been more relevant in the aftermath of *Brown v. Board of Education*. Nelle knew her Bible.

Go Set a Watchman also belongs to the literary tradition of Christian allegory set in the racially turbulent 1950s. In the beginning, Eden is a garden of childlike innocence where we believe our parents are perfect. Then children grow older and judge their parents more harshly. Often they forgive them. Sometimes, they do not. In her mid-twenties, living far from Alabama where she had been inoculated to some extent against the state's incestuous and enforced conformity by reading almost weekly in the *New York Times* of yet another racist outrage by "her people," Nelle's rage finally spilled over.

Despite a cast of characters and places familiar to those who first read *Mockingbird*—for instance in *Watchman*, Jean Louise revisits Finch's Landing, swims nude with her fiancé, looks upriver from the bluff, and imagines once more childhood stories of the canoe fight where Sam Dale "fit" the Indians—the Maycomb Nelle depicts in *Watchman* has gone haywire. Jean Louise departs the Sunday morning worship service for lunch where she learns of a meeting to be held in the courthouse. With nothing better to do on a Sunday afternoon in the tiny town, she slips into the segregated balcony unnoticed—the same balcony from which as Scout in *Mockingbird* she, her brother, and friend Dill will witness her father's heroic defense of Tom Robinson—and listens instead to her father and fiancé denounce the *Brown v. Board* Supreme Court decision and other threats to apartheid. Their accommodationist "triumph" for the Sunday afternoon is keeping the Ku Klux Klan out of town by establishing a chapter of the less violent but equally racist White Citizens Council. Having lost her childhood innocence about her father and boyfriend in a single afternoon, the rest of the novel is a profane denunciation of the two men who mattered most in her life. In the end, she breaks her engagement and returns to New York City, although with some understanding of how people have to compromise in order to preserve family ties and home places.

Her beloved C. S. Lewis would have described *Watchman* as a traditional Christian allegory: childhood innocence; her father's fall from grace; judgmentalism; a fractured community; ending in some form of forgiveness and reconciliation. Gone forever are the idyllic and naïve illusions of childhood.

BOTH LITERARY AND HISTORICAL critics of the idealistic depiction of Atticus Finch in *To Kill a Mockingbird* can read their fill of denunciation of him in Harper Lee's first-written manuscript, *Go Set a Watchman*. They probably would have concluded, as Dartie and I did, that Nelle included more invective in *Watchman* than any refined work of fiction can absorb. Editor Tay Hohoff certainly believed it was not fine writing. Perhaps Hohoff also decided America was not ready for this novel in 1957.

Meanwhile, in Nelle's home state, two teenage Baptist boys were preaching while she was writing. We were both sons and grandsons of sharecroppers, born nine months apart in 1940. John Lewis lived in Pike County and at the time I lived in Houston, one county to the south. Baptists of both races then required nothing of preacher boys beyond testimony of conversion, a divine "calling" to preach, and some evidence of that calling from the pulpit. John had an advantage over me in the pulpit. Whereas I had limited opportunities to preach at interdenominational "Youth for Christ" rallies and on Youth Sunday at Calvary Baptist Church in Dothan, John joked that he had an uncritical congregation of chickens in his yard to practice on. I studied the Bible just as seriously as he did, noting that the second most frequent theme in the book after idolatry was justice for the poor and oppressed, a conclusion John and I reached about the same time. Despite contrary pressure from my culture, I felt the liberating power of Scripture peeling away my racial and class perceptions like layers of white skin burned by too much sun during Alabama summers. John went on to a black Baptist college in Nashville and I to a white Baptist college in Birmingham. He graduated to lunch-counter sit-ins in Nashville. I progressed a few years behind him, while in graduate school, to a boycott of The Mecca next to the Florida State University campus because it refused to serve our first black students, withdrawing Dartie's and my church memberships from Tallahassee's First Baptist Church for the same reason.

During those years, my father and I had more than one heated conversation about race, though none as profane and colorful as the vocabulary Nelle had picked up in New York City. However, I was every bit as sanctimonious as Jean Louise Finch, an attitude I now regret. Charge it to youthful arrogance.

Late in life, Dad mellowed and transcended his own childhood as much as I did mine. He served a term as president of the Pinson Kiwanis Club in a mostly white town next door to north Birmingham, where my mother was a beloved fourth grade teacher. One day one of her students told her that the KKK was going to burn a cross in her yard. "Why would they do that?" she asked. "Because Mr. Flynt won't allow a Ku Klux Klan rally at the Kiwanis Club Park," the innocent youngster answered. Mom explained that he did not make such decisions. The club did not allow any group to use the park without a vote of every member. That was not entirely true, but it may have saved some Klansman's life. Dad was hot-tempered and had an array of guns to protect him from varmints, whether animal or human. Like Nelle's father's for her, Dad's love for me was unconditional, however much we clashed about race. And as he aged and America changed, he changed too, though never as much as I did. Nelle relished that story. When Dartie and I read *Watchman*, I understood why.

ON FEBRUARY 3, 2015, while listening to National Public Radio in my car, the two lead news stories dealt with Alabama. The Eleventh United States Circuit Court in Atlanta had upheld a ruling by a judge in Mobile striking down Alabama's ban on same-sex marriages, and a new novel by Harper Lee had been discovered. I hurried into the house to share the news with Dartie. She was as befuddled by the book news as I was. The former story had a short life. The Harper Lee story sucked the oxygen out of cultural news in the English-speaking world for months to come. Within minutes a reporter for NPR called. It was my third conversation with her. The first was the day she asked me to record an anticipatory obituary for Harper Lee, a not uncommon media request about aging celebrities. When news of Harper's stroke leaked to the public, the NPR reporter called me to update the obituary that was being held in reserve.

The ensuing media avalanche mostly dealt with the same questions. Where had the manuscript been for six decades? It seemed too coincidental that Tonja Carter had found the manuscript while going through papers in Alice Lee's office shortly after Alice's death in November 2014. Because Carter held Harper Lee's power of attorney but would not allow a press conference or explain where the manuscript had been, could I confirm that Lee had given her consent for publication? Would the publication of a possibly inferior new novel tarnish her literary reputation? Having refused to write another novel for all these years, why allow one to be published now?

Between Tuesday, February 3 and Saturday, February 7, I recorded in my journal a partial list of reporters who called and their outlets: all major Alabama newspapers; five London-based papers; the *Wall Street Journal*, *Washington Post*, and *New York Times*; and news programs on MSNBC, CBS, NBC, and ABC.

I patiently explained that Dartie and I had visited Nelle the day before the story broke, she had not mentioned it, but was in good spirits, alert and talkative. I noted that Monroeville gossip about dementia, incapacity to give informed consent, and allegations of manipulation were the sort of things that were often read into the normal memory problems of an eighty-nine-year-old deaf person who also suffered from macular degeneration. None of the local residents discussing her condition—and talking to the media—had access to Harper Lee, I emphasized.

I called Nelle's nephew Hank Conner to ask what had happened. He told me that he had read the "Watchman" manuscript in the late 1950s while visiting his grandfather in Monroeville and did not much like it. When he learned that Nelle had agreed to its publication, he had driven to Monroeville and asked her numerous times over two days (partly because of her hearing difficulty but perhaps also because of rumored dementia) if she really wanted the book published. She not only affirmed her decision but became aggravated at his repetitive interrogation.

I suggested to Tonja that she hold a press conference to explain where the manuscript had been all these years, when and how it had been discovered, and the decision to publish it. Having only recently become head of the Lee law firm, being involved in a suit against the museum, being an "outsider" by Monroeville's definition, and having almost no experience with the national press, she perceived sharks circling around her and consented only to an email interview with the *New York Times*. This at least moved the conversation temporarily onto the novel and away from conspiracy theories.

Fed up with that line of questioning myself, and beginning to feel as though Dartie and I were being dragged into the media frenzy because we refused to confirm falsely that Nelle suffered from dementia, we began to have our own issues with the town. If local people had evidence of mental illness or of a conspiracy by Carter, Harper Lee's agent in London, her publisher, or anyone else, they should file formal charges with appropriate agencies such as the Alabama Bar Association, Adult Protective Services, or the local police. Which is what someone did. We drove to Monroeville on February 9 to assess matters for ourselves. Everything had changed since our visit a week earlier. As we drove into The Meadows' parking lot, a state car from the elder abuse agency blocked access. Someone had already filed criminal charges that Nelle had been abused. An officer asked for our identification and who we had come to visit. He then escorted us into the building. The residents were huddled together in the commons room, which was as quiet as a morgue. The usual smiles and laughter had vanished. Even the staff was silent and made no eye contact with us.

We acted as we always did, greeting residents and staff. They were relieved when I pushed her wheelchair into her apartment, which consisted of two small rooms and a bathroom. When we arrived, I asked Nelle about her new novel. "What new novel?" she replied. Her answer momentarily stunned us. I answered, "*Go Set a Watchman*, the novel the entire nation is talking about." She replied with a wicked smile as if she had been setting up this conversation all day: "Oh, that's not my new novel. That's my old novel." "Well, old or new," I replied with relief, "it's number one on Amazon's advance order list." "You lie!" she replied as we slid into a cycle of trading twelves. "I do not lie, Nelle. I am a Baptist minister." "That makes it even worse," she snickered. "You are too smart to be a Baptist preacher."

I changed the subject because I was in no mood for trading twelves that day. "You should be so proud, Nelle. This is the most important literary event in decades!" Following a pause, she responded in almost a whisper, shoulders sagging and staring at her feet, "I'm not so sure anymore."

Noting her sudden mood change, we retreated to our repertoire of Little Harper stories until she began laughing again. The cliché may be true that God gives us memory so we can know what roses smell like in December. But that afternoon we tried to forget about the furor over *Watchman* and what Dartie called "the weeks of the ravenous wolves": New York City conspiracy theorists; Monroeville gossips; a frail, elderly woman caught up in a formal criminal investigation.

BEFORE LEAVING FOR HOME, we offered our support to The Meadows' director. She complained that appropriate care for all the residents was affected by what was happening. Even Tonja had flared up at her. Overwhelmed by national and even international scrutiny and elder abuse charges, the director angrily told Tonja that she had twelve residents to care for, not just Harper Lee. If Tonja wanted to take Harper somewhere else, that was fine with her. We realized we had blundered into a storm, wished her well, volunteered to testify about the staff's professionalism and quality care should there be further investigations, and departed for Auburn. On the trip home we were as quiet and depressed as The Meadows staff had been.

Fortunately, our help was not needed. The investigation revealed no abuse except what Nelle meted out to her interrogators. She told state investigators, "Go to hell and leave me alone."

Apparently that outburst persuaded them she was in possession of her faculties, and all charges were dismissed. Most of the allegations had derived from national conspiracy theories, local gossip, and some writers with their own agendas. National media coverage tended to be one-sided because no alternative narrative emerged other than mine, which only achieved credibility months later when I was conducting my own news conferences in the run-up to the release of *Watchman*. Not wanting to find fault with one of their own, lots of Monroeville residents blamed Tonja Carter for Nelle's idiosyncrasies, grievances, and fury at the invasion of her privacy. They did not comprehend that extreme privacy had been Nelle's lifestyle since leaving Alabama in 1949 and she did not intend to relinquish it as long as she drew breath. She was living in Monroeville because returning to the life she remembered would have been difficult at best. Alice was near one hundred and growing frail, and she had pressed Nelle to return to Monroeville.

Soon enough this episode was swallowed by the media extravaganza surrounding publication of *Go Set a Watchman*. On February 12, after breakfast with friends in Montgomery, we returned home at noon to a ringing telephone. Whenever I replaced the phone in its cradle, it rang again. Except for one desperate bathroom break, I was on the phone continuously until we left for our midweek church service at 5:30. As we walked out the door, I noticed that we had eleven phone messages. We returned at 7 o'clock to a ringing telephone. The calls continued without a break until 10 p.m. when I took the phone off its cradle and we fell into exhausted sleep. I had spent eight hours talking with reporters and my ear was numb.

A month later, after lecturing on the coast to the Alabama

College English Teachers Association about the emerging *Watchman* phenomenon, we bought Key lime pies for the residents and staff of The Meadows and delivered them on the way home. Nelle welcomed the pie but refused to use her hearing aid or talk about *Watchman*. I joked that at least she would make lots of money. She shrugged, "I doubt anyone will read it."

She was mistaken. I logged twenty more calls in my journal as publishing day approached, from papers as diverse as the *Guardian* in London and the *New York Times*, mostly asking about Nelle's memory and cognitive ability. I told callers that I was not a neurologist but if they knew some good ones, send them to Monroeville because the town was suffering from mass hysteria.

On our next visit we carried Nelle a list of best-selling books on which *Mockingbird* had risen to fourteenth in its fifty-fifth year of educating and entertaining the world. Nelle was more interested in the humorous sketch of her father in the 1927 Alabama legislature which a friend had let me borrow. I had also found an historical sketch of the 15th Alabama Regiment in which her grandfather had served at Gettysburg.

Gradually and with the end of the elder abuse investigation the mini-drama of the new book and press attention subsided. Our writer son, Sean, sent us a masterful summary of that winter and spring:

> So many people who claim to love *Mockingbird* have either forgotten the point or never got it. They'll drag her out into the spotlight even if it kills her just so they can satisfy their curiosity. Reminds me of a fourth-grade demonstration of a tortoise's beating heart. We saw it beat. The tortoise died.

Our next visit with Nelle, on April 5, 2015, continued the alternating cycle of good and bad days. It was a particularly upbeat day. She was taking her allergy medication and using her hearing aid. She entertained us with another lengthy recitation of the Maxwell murder, naming his wives and the reporter for the local paper whom she had interviewed. As an afterthought, she hoped she had sent a copy of "The Reverend" and "Watchman" manuscripts to Alice. We had brought her a short article from *The Economist* about her soon-to-be-published novel. She dismissed the article: "I can't remember that book. I wrote it years ago . . ." That was our first indication that she had made no revisions for publication. We joked, traded twelves, and talked for more than an hour, relieved both by her mental acuity and momentary good humor.

IN LATE APRIL 2015 we returned to Monroeville for the annual Alabama Writers Symposium and my interview with journalist and television host Katie Couric. Tonja Carter had written me that she and Andrew Nurnberg, Harper Lee's then international agent, thought it best if I read *Go Set a Watchman* before the interview. After picking up Tonja's copy at her office, Dartie and I discussed who should read it first.

Obviously we were both eager after months of speculation, media controversy, and publisher hype. But I had the Couric interview early the next morning. In a marriage, this is called a disagreement. Philosophers and theologians refer to it as an "existential crisis." Dartie had priority of age. I had priority of interview. I toyed with suggesting that if she had first option, my legendarily private spouse should also substitute for me in the Couric interview. But calling her bluff could be risky. She was smart, articulate, a skilled actor, knew Nelle as well or better than I did, and could have carried off the interview flawlessly. Better try another strategy, I concluded.

I volunteered to read the manuscript aloud so we could experience it at the same time. We skipped dinner, and I began reading mid-afternoon. By 3 a.m. I was too exhausted and hoarse to continue, and I still had fifty pages to go. Dartie took mercy on me (partly because the profane denunciation of Harper's relatives became redundant) and turned off the bed light while I quickly and silently finished reading by the light on the table. The strident and denunciatory language was foreign to Dartie's upbringing in a pious Baptist preacher's family though not to mine. She had undoubtedly read all these words in her voracious reading of fiction but probably not quite so concentrated in one novel. I was not surprised. My father had just as colorful a vocabulary when angry, and I had my own occasional problems with anger management although I had never "cussed" my father, as we say in the South.

As I turned in for a few hours' sleep before my interview, I pondered other directions in which Tay Hohoff could have steered this manuscript. It could have become a premier "race novel" in 1960. Much of American literature from Mark Twain forward dealt with race. But a "race novel" moves beyond plot. The author's intent is to affect laws, practices, and attitudes, to prevent racial violence, to alter belief systems tracking from slavery to apartheid to informal systems of injustice. Given the historical context in which Nelle wrote the novel in the mid-1950s, I had no problem conceiving of it as one of the nation's early "race novels" from the perspective of internal racial debates within white families, however flawed it was as literature.

During a groggy, sleep-deprived breakfast, Dartie and I talked about *Watchman*. Harper was in her late twenties when she wrote it, barely thirty when she submitted it to Hohoff. She wrote from the same subterranean rage we had felt when our Baptist church in Tallahassee, Florida, voted against admitting African Americans to our worship services. I had heaped similar abuse on my father. Unlike Atticus, he had dumped it back on me. I avoided Jean Louise's profanity but not her judgmentalism.

By the time *Watchman* was published sixty years later, it seemed more a relic of another age than a relevant discussion of race in America. But published in 1960, it would have had a significant relevance as a symbol of generational differences. I compared the novel to a contemporary book, Martha Nussbaum's *Anger and Forgiveness*. Nussbaum argues that anger can be good or bad. If anger results in revenge, retribution, payback for grievances, and alienation, as it often does in the Bible, it is a negative life force. But if anger can be harnessed toward justice, rule of law, welfare of others, new beginnings, and reconciliation, it can be a powerful force for healing. That is also in the Bible.

Of course I could not cite details of the not yet publicly released *Watchman* to Couric, but I could probe Christian theology of generational division and reconciliation already revealed in HarperCollins' advance publicity. Placing modern fiction into a religious context in a nation where biblical literacy is roughly equivalent to public understanding of quasars seemed futile, but I tried anyway.

WHETHER READ ALOUD OR silently, the novel's flaws are obvious. *Watchman* may contain a more honest appraisal than *Mockingbird* did of her father's complicity in apartheid and her own racial sensibilities in the mid-1950s. Yet literary critics and some historians persist in emphasizing Harper Lee's idealized 1960 portrayal of Atticus Finch in *Mockingbird* as if it is the definitive fictional version of her father, while ignoring her evisceration of him in *Watchman* three years earlier.

Inattention to *Watchman* also masks the critical role Hohoff played in turning a decent but racist man into a saintly father. There is no definitive explanation of how or why Hohoff helped shift the focus of Lee's writing. Did Hohoff conclude in 1957, in the aftermath of the 1954 *Brown v. Board of Education* decision that most readers, North and South, were not yet ready for a bright, racially enlightened Southern expatriate daughter verbally abusing her father and hometown? Or did she simply conclude that the novel was badly written? At any rate, under Hohoff's careful tutelage, Nelle set about writing a different book, not the story of a rebellious, twenty-something, angry daughter but the tale of three precocious children experiencing their initial disillusionment with the adult world. Fortunately, both editor Hohoff and agent Maurice Crain left tantalizing hints. *Mockingbird* publisher J. B. Lippincott published its own chronicle, *The Author and His Audience,* for the company's 175th birthday in 1967. The thin volume included an essay by Hohoff about *Watchman*'s three-year transformation into *Mockingbird*. Here is a lengthy excerpt:

> First of all, the element in the original manuscript which was unmistakable: it was alive, the characters stood on their own two feet, they were three-dimensional. And the spark of the true writer flashed in every line.

Though Miss Lee had then never published even an essay or a short story, this was clearly not the work of an amateur or tyro [beginner]. And indeed, she had written constantly since her very early childhood. It was difficult at first to understand why she had resisted the temptation to try, at least, for publication, but as I grew to know her better, I came to believe the cause lay in an innate humility and a deep respect for the art of writing. To put it another way, what she wanted with all her being was to *write*—not merely to "be a writer." She had learned the essential part of her craft, with no so-called professional help, simply by working at it and working at it, endlessly.

However, the manuscript we saw was more a series of anecdotes than a fully conceived novel. The editorial call to duty was plain. She needed, at last, professional help in organizing her material and developing a sound plot structure.

After a couple of false starts, the story-line, interplay of characters, and fall of emphasis grew clearer, and with each revision—there were many minor changes as the story grew in strength and in her own vision of it—the true stature of the novel became evident.

We saw a great deal of each other during this period, and, if conditions make it possible, I believe such close, frequent communication can be of enormous benefit to the author, the book, and incidentally to the editor. But of course writing is the loneliest of activities. Harper Lee literally spent her days and nights in the most intense efforts to set down what she wanted to say in the way which would best say it to a reader. You ask for "chapter and verse." That's a bit hard. It's no secret that she was living on next to nothing and in considerable physical discomfort while she was writing *Mockingbird*. I don't think anyone, certainly not I, ever heard one small mutter of discontent throughout all those months of writing and tearing up, writing and tearing up.

And you ask how she responded to my criticisms. Well, with intelligence, naturally, but one expects that, never mind how often one may be disappointed. When she disagreed with a suggestion, we talked it out, sometimes for hours. And sometimes she came around to my way of thinking, sometimes I to hers, sometimes the discussion would open up an entirely new line of country [sic]. I think I can say with truth that she always knew I was in her corner, even when I was most critical, which is really all there is to say about the editor's part in the success of *Mockingbird*. As you know, the sole function of an editor is to help a writer bring forth the best book in him. Unless a writer will totally commit himself to the same end, the editor must be content with mid-wifing a disappointingly puny child. It is because, and only because, Harper Lee did so totally commit herself that *Mockingbird* reveals a remarkable talent at its (then) best.

Maurice Crain offered a briefer summary for a local newspaper in the 1960s:

> Most good books ... are ones that have been a long time maturing, with a lot of cutting and fitting and replanning done along the way. Mockingbird, for instance, was about the most replanned and rewritten book I ever had a hand in and it turned out finally that all the labor on it was well justified, and if the Lippincott editors hadn't been so fussy and painstaking we wouldn't have had nearly so good a book.

When I arrived at the Monroe County courthouse, the contradictions of venue and occasion flooded over me. The courtroom on the second floor was probably the most recognizable legal venue on earth thanks to her novel and the movie. This amused Nelle, because what made the courthouse famous was fictional, and the movie was not actually filmed there. As I walked in, the courtroom was nearly unrecognizable. Three camera and sound crews, plus all their equipment, had transformed its iconic grandeur into a studio. Couric had interviewed various conspiracy theorists anxious to deflect attention from Nelle to her lawyer. This required all sorts of collateral hypotheses: that Nelle was daft; that Monroeville's middle class, consisting of people such as A. C. Lee, had not been racists in the 1960s; that Nelle adored her small hometown. So far as we knew, none of this was true.

Furthermore, I had recently finished *Alabama in the Twentieth Century*, a book for which Nelle had written a blurb, that contained a chapter about African Americans, racism, discrimination, and the politics of black and poor white voter suppression enshrined in the 1901 Constitution. My historical documentation bore more resemblance to *Watchman*'s Alabama than to *Mockingbird*'s. I remembered Nelle's commentary: "Same damned town, same damned people I wrote about in *Mockingbird*." I could have added, if local folks are upset now, wait until they read *Watchman*.

Before the interview, Couric and I talked a long time about happier topics, her mother and father who are buried in Eufaula near Louise Conner, and her cousins who lived in Alexander City. She was so excellent, empathetic, and charming an interviewer that I hated to inject a dose of reality when she asked if I could arrange an interview with Nelle. I explained that Dartie and I were only her friends, not her attorney or agent, so permitting interviews was not part of our job description. Furthermore, her tiny apartment in The Meadows barely had room for Nelle, Dartie, and me and was entirely too small for Couric, a camera crew, sound equipment, and Harper Lee. Also, a security guard now blocked access. The day before, the guard had turned away a reporter for *El Pais*, one of the world's premier Spanish-language newspapers, who tried to gain entrance despite my warning that it would not be permitted.

I tried to imagine the chaos of the normally tranquil The Meadows if the famous Katie Couric arrived with part of her entourage in tow after months of allegations of abuse and outside investigators. If charm could have spun a miracle, Couric would have made it in. Unfortunately for her, Tonja, Nelle, and the director of The Meadows were well beyond charm campaigns by this juncture. When we told Nelle about my interview with Couric and my deflection of the film crew, she offered two words either to me or the deity: "Thank God!"

Between May 25 and the release of *Watchman* on July 4, Nelle's life consisted of the usual solitary boredom while Dartie's and my life spun into media chaos. My rule was not to answer questions about Nelle's private life beyond a non-neurological opinion that she had the same sort of memory issues any octogenarian usually had but was lucid and did not appear to have dementia except on days when she could not hear.

As publication day neared, the frenzied pace of interviews accelerated. Nelle, Tonja, Dartie, and Andrew Nurnberg were silent. That left me talking. Tonya Gold, a British reporter for

London's *Sunday Times*, brought a documentary photographer and stayed for a day before departing to Monroeville. I thought her subsequent article was the fairest and best essay published about Nelle and her new book. A reporter for *Der Spiegel* followed closely behind. A team from Australian public television filmed for another half day. I spent portions of an afternoon in a phone interview (which I had come to hate) talking with Lucia Benavente of RCN Radio in Colombia. CBS and *Wall Street Journal* reporters split another half day. On July 3 we finally received our own advance copy of *Go Set a Watchman* from HarperCollins. That allowed me more meticulous preparation for the extravaganza that followed on July 13–15, 2015, in Monroeville.

The first event was an interview with PBS NewsHour in tandem with Natasha Treathewey, an old friend from our time together on the Auburn faculty and a Pulitzer Prize-winning poet. Ed Lavandera, my favorite CNN interviewer for his wonderful coverage of the South, was next, followed by Rick McKay of Reuters and Tom Ashbrook of NPR On-Point. That all preceded a press conference with forty reporters from countries across the globe. When I arrived back at the motel, Dartie asked how things had gone. I remembered and identified with an Abraham Lincoln story about a nonconformist who had been tarred and feathered: "If it had not been for the honor of the whole thing, I had just as soon passed it up." More seriously, I told her what an impossible ordeal the day would have been for her or Nelle. I did meet an old friend, Lee Sentell, the best tourism director the state of Alabama ever had, who told me he was going to pay for our motel room because for the next two days Harper Lee would be Alabama's leading tourist attraction. He was not wrong!

Late that afternoon we slipped the grasp of reporters in order to report to the one who really mattered. We took Nelle a thick file of pre-publication reviews from newspapers such as the *Wall Street Journal*, *New York Times*, the *Spectator* in London, and numerous Alabama papers. The *New York Times* review was unprecedented not so much for the review itself as for its presence on page one. "You lie!" she shouted when I told her of its location. Beyond all the controversy of the past six months, from which she had been carefully and thoroughly shielded, and her own nonchalance, we realized that at last she fully understood her status as one of the world's most important literary figures and was genuinely excited.

That evening we shared dinner with our friend and Harper Lee scholar, Nancy Anderson. She and her husband Rick had just returned from Ireland and had a story and photograph to pass along to Nelle. The window of Hodges Figg's Book Shoppe in Dublin (the nation's oldest, opened in 1768, and mentioned in James Joyce's *Ulysses*) contained stacks of *Mockingbird* and *Watchman* and displayed covers of both. When we told Harper Nancy's story the next day, it was one of the infrequent occasions when she did not dismiss her fame with jocularity, hyperbole, or denial. What could she say? She simply retreated into her own reverie.

Thousands of people crowded Monroeville's Ole Curiosity Book Shoppe that day at noon to drink champagne (I had a glass for Nelle's sake while Dartie stood by her Baptist convictions), toast Harper Lee, listen to an actor portraying Atticus Finch, and purchase books. The day was more carnival than book release. We met people from Wales, Italy, and most American states. Some had flown in from the West Coast. I spent most of the day in more press conferences as the undelegated family spokesman. When we visited Nelle late that afternoon to summarize the festivities, she was attentive, talkative, jovial, coy, and excited. It probably was the best day of our decade-long friendship. Dartie set the mood by describing visitors from throughout the world. I told the more exciting news—to her—how much money she was going to make. HarperCollins announced that her pre-publication first-day sales of more than seven hundred thousand copies was a publishing record. Books-a-Million and Barnes and Noble, the nation's largest retail chain stores, also had broken one-day record sales of a book.

Nelle grinned: "I am a very rich woman!" Dartie amended her self-congratulatory pronouncement: "Nelle, you have been a very rich woman for a very long time!" First-week sales of 1.1 million copies set yet another American record for a novel. Nelle's gloom over Alice's death and the ruckus over *Watchman* steadily faded during America's new romance with Harper Lee.

DESPITE TONJA'S EFFORTS, NOT much had changed in Monroeville. Someone reported that her restaurant was selling liquor to minors in carry-out containers. The resulting investigation uncovered no evidence of such violations. When Nelle learned of the charges, she was appalled, congratulating Tonja for fighting back: "Kid, you are my Atticus!" Tonja replied: "I feel more like your Tom Robinson!"

Many readers were disappointed by *Watchman*'s language, setting, subject, and writing. Critics generally agreed that the book had diminished her literary reputation. One critic groused that Harper Lee minus Tay Hohoff equaled mediocrity. They dismissed her sanctimonious dialogue, uneven characterizations, and lack of polish. Many liberal Northern readers were appalled at the main character's reconciliation with her father and uncle. Many Southern readers preferred the childhood innocence of *Mockingbird* and questioned why Harper had ripped the scabs off so many wounds.

We defended the novel in two ways. Don't compare it to *Mockingbird*. Think of it as Claude Monet's first shimmering impressionist painting of French coastal towns in the 1860s, not the blossoming of Impressionism decades later. If you want to understand the latter, you have to study both periods. My rebuttal to fellow Southerners was that wounds seldom heal completely until scabs come off. In addition, one close New York friend told us that she believed the accommodationist ending of *Watchman* was closer to Harper's gradualist approach to ending segregation in the 1950s than her denunciation of her father.

No novel I remembered from the 1950s other than *Invisible Man* had penetrated so deeply into the tangled web of race, family, and community. Jean Louise's denunciation of her father's racism was courageous. She did not bother with defenses of his essential decency or Methodist piety, his civic virtue or his good-neighborliness. She fearlessly cut right to the heart of his racist assumptions, however exemplary a citizen and father he might be. The historian in me pondered silently—for there was no reason amidst her satisfaction with her continuing celebrity to mention it—how different America might have been in the twenty-first century if all its sons and daughters who thought like Jean Louise Finch in 1957 had debated these issues with their parents.

OUR VISIT IN NOVEMBER after the frantic events of Spring and Summer had swept past was a shuddering contrast. Tonja Carter's husband, Patrick, a retired Delta Airlines pilot, had been killed while flying a World War I vintage biplane to Alabama. She and the children were devastated. The youngest had just begun her freshman year at Auburn, and we had pledged to help her through the inevitable tough transition. I was a minister who had both studied and experienced grief. The Carters were Catholic, so I took them a copy of one of my favorite books about grief and recovery, Catholic priest Henri Nouwen's *Turn My Mourning Into Dancing*. I explained to Tonja and the children that although Monroeville had chosen Tonja as the villain in the *Watchman* saga, we were glad the novel had been found and published. As we drove home, Dartie and I discussed how suddenly human tragedy can displace controversies that had seemed of such transcendent importance.

Many months after publication of *Watchman*, I received an insightful letter from Methodist minister Ray E. Whatley, who had pastored the Lee family church from 1951 to 1953. When first assigned, it seemed a perfect match of preacher and parish. Whatley was born twenty-eight miles from Monroeville in a Black Belt community bearing his family name.

Although many ambitious young ministers would have considered both church and town part of Alabama's backwater, Whatley was not one of them. And unlike many white communities where Methodist domination in the nineteenth century had been displaced by Baptists in the twentieth, Methodists maintained their hegemony in Monroeville. J. B. Barnett was president of Monroe County Bank and a director of two other financial institutions. He also had been senior partner in the law firm Barnett, Bug, and Lee when Harper's father was a junior partner. Their law offices were just around the square from the town's newspaper owned by

A. C. Lee. Another prominent Methodist layman served as long-time circuit judge of Monroe and two adjacent counties.

Reverend Whatley was the youngest pastor to serve Monroeville Methodist Church during Nelle's lifetime and was imprinted by the racial and political liberalism about to disrupt Southern Methodism, particularly on racial matters. Like me, he had been influenced by the teachings of the "Social Gospel" in college and divinity school.

Nelle's father served seven years as chairman of the church board and of the pastoral relations committee, including all three years of Whatley's term as pastor. He privately scolded the young pastor for straying too far from personal evangelism into controversial social issues. A. C. and Alice also opposed merging the Central Alabama (African American) Conference of the United Methodists with its white Alabama brothers and sisters. Whatley favored integrating them. He defended his preaching to me, noting that the church added more members during his tenure than any ensuing pastorate during the following forty years. He also confirmed that he was the most liberal pastor on social issues, which he believed was the actual grievance A. C. Lee and other prominent lay leaders had with him.

Partly as a result of Coley Lee's criticism, the bishop reassigned Whatley to St. Mark's Methodist Church in downtown Montgomery, located a block from the Alabama governor's mansion soon to be occupied by George Wallace. In 1955, while pastor of St. Mark's, Whatley helped organize, and was elected president of the Montgomery chapter of the liberal Alabama Council on Human Relations. Martin Luther King Jr., the new pastor of Dexter Avenue Baptist Church, was elected vice president.

Whatley noted that Nelle was unaware of the details of the Monroeville church controversy, which was fairly tightly contained. She lived in New York City, was working on *Watchman*, seldom returned home, and when she did rarely attended church. Although at the time Whatley knew nothing about *Watchman's* existence, he once spoke to her when both returned to Monroeville for visits, admonishing her that "young people should stand on the shoulders of their elders . . . not kick their heads. They were our parents and we respected them whether we agreed with them or not."

He later read *Watchman* and did not approve of its profane denunciation of the fictional father who in real life had him removed as pastor, although he considered the novel "a powerful story illustrating the intensity of the struggles of the fifties . . . about which people who did not live in the South back then needed to know." He even identified for me the probable fictional racist demagogue who harangued the white male courthouse audience in *Watchman* as Macon County cotton planter and Alabama State Senator Sam Engelhardt, a White Citizens Council leader who—Whatley believed—had pressured the Methodist bishop to deny Whatley two other Black Belt pastorates.

Whatley read in *Watchman* a daughter's disillusionment with her father's racism during the tumultuous events of the 1950s. He emphasized the pernicious way otherwise godly people distorted the Bible into a defense of apartheid: "People who think that a lawyer, who would have defended a black man in court meant the lawyer was opposed to segregation, do not understand Alabama society of the early 1950s. Atticus tries to explain [in *Watchman*] his position based on the sincerely held belief that

Negro people were an inferior . . . race incapable of much more than menial labor and [serving] white people and not capable of governing themselves." He ended his letter sardonically: "But it's in the Bible! Yes, they were supported by the curse of Ham in Genesis 9: 20–27."

Whatley speculated that Alice Lee's devotion to her father and reluctance to allow the world to read Nelle's denunciation of him in *Watchman* explained why she sealed it away until after her death. Suddenly, that made sense to us. Tonja's primary fiduciary responsibility was maximizing her client's portfolio, not protecting the image of a fictional father. Nelle had forgotten about the novel. Alice had not.

In his remarkably forgiving and reconciling letter, Whatley praised Alice's maturing racial sensibilities. She had been a Methodist pioneer on behalf of women ministers and had promoted lay women's leadership both in the South Alabama-West Florida Conference and nationally. Eventually she played a leading role in integrating black and white Methodist conferences in Alabama. Whatley also remained close to Louise Conner, who sometimes hosted the Whatleys in her home after he left Monroeville.

His conclusion to me was that Methodists could sharply disagree on matters of race, that "gradualism," though not his preference, led to change, although much too slowly. Dartie and I marveled at his civility and kind spirit which seemed as much an illusion in twenty-first century America as it must have been in 1950s Monroeville.

OF THE MANY BOOKS we had read during childhood, Nelle, Dartie and I had some in common, including John Bunyan's *Pilgrim's*

Progress. A Christian allegory written in 1678 while Bunyan was imprisoned for conducting unsanctioned religious services, the book is still regarded as one of the most important works of theological fiction in English literature. Some scholars consider it the first English novel. The story compares the importance of home, journey, and destination ("the celestial city") in the human odyssey. It has been translated into two hundred languages and has never been out of print.

Among recent American writers, Pulitzer Prize-winner Marilynne Robinson has most brilliantly explored the same terrain in her trilogy, *Gilead, Home,* and *Lila.* The Presbyterian pastor in the trilogy tells his son Jack, "It is in family that we most often feel the grace of God, His faithfulness." His daughter Glory, torn between her father's piety and the stifling boredom of Gilead, her hometown, and the exciting big city world beyond its boundaries, sounds like Nelle describing Monroeville in 1957 where every day lasted twenty-four hours but seemed much longer: "Gilead, Gilead, dreaming out its curse of sameness, somnolence. 'How could anyone live here?' That was the question [the children] asked one another, out of their father's hearing, when they came back from college, or from the world. Why should anyone stay?"

In Robinson's fiction, "home" is a profound theological destination: "Weary or bitter or bewildered as we may be, God is faithful. He lets us wander so we will know what it means to come home."

In many ways, *Go Set a Watchman* deals with the same literary space as Bunyan and Robinson but from an entirely different theological perspective. It remains rooted in an earlier age of American religion, ethics, and family values complete with

Christian metaphors such as a prophetic "watchman" and a prodigal daughter who leaves home for brighter lights and secular excitement, then revisits home to find some reason to stay. But Jean Louise's fictional return home does not go well. Rather than reclaiming the innocence of childhood, she discovers the full extent of adult family bigotry, her father's cultural captivity to intolerance and flawed community values rather than his heroism. She makes her recently acquired racial enlightenment normative for her benighted family and acquaintances, even though they were born in an earlier time and must survive in a different culture. Her enlightenment does not trigger a return home but a permanent separation from it. What to her is "righteous" is to them "self-righteous." At the end of the novel, Jean Louise is reconciled to family and their continuing love for her, but she also realizes that their differences make "home" an impossible destination for her. Both destination and home became New York City. Reconciliation with family is possible, reconciliation with Maycomb impossible. Idealism and youthful visions take her back to New York City where she "belongs." Only the exigency of her father's frailty and aging in 1960–1962, followed by her own nearly a half century later would bring the author back to a flawed place that could never be her real home again.

Finis

IN SOME WAYS, NELLE HARPER LEE OCCUPIED THREE WORLDS, one psychological, another social, and the final one literary. Alabama mostly nourished her, but New York City shaped her. In the end, *To Kill a Mockingbird* and *Go Set a Watchman* as her literary heritage were fusions of both worlds. Some of her happiest days were spent at the University of Alabama where she disdained its frivolous sorority life in preference for animated arguments with friends on the staff of the *Rammer Jammer*. If she had a hero beyond her father, brother, and sisters, it was Paul "Bear" Bryant. As a brilliant woman who could quote long passages of Shakespeare until her death at age eighty-nine, she could also trump the Bard with a silly jingle from her undergraduate adulation of the Crimson Tide.

As arguably America's most beloved writer of arguably the world's favorite novel, she could have sprouted an ego the size of Mount Rushmore. Instead, she lived an intensely private life filled with books, theater, sports, and close friends. A small-town girl and a global celebrity, she craved the anonymity of America's largest city. Despite the adoration in her hometown and state, her closest friends were a mixture of Alabamians, New Yorkers, and even Kansans.

Truman Capote's early friendship turned out to be as much a curse as a blessing. His brilliance, egotism, lifestyle, and jealousy were poisonous weeds killing every relationship in their vicinity. His genius also multiplied her insecurities. Who could steer a canoe in the wake of his literary battleship? If she initially hesitated to deliver a typed copy of *Mockingbird* to Maurice Crain or to send forth a manuscript of "The Reverend" after the deaths of Crain and Hohoff, who could blame her? Some writers need cheerleaders to validate their talent. Others need great editors. Harper needed both and after 1970 had neither.

Pulitzer Prize-winner Annie Dillard, a brilliant writer about the natural world, never figured out why mockingbirds sing. Or exactly what they sing. Dartie never worried about why or what; she was a solitary "birder" content to watch them with binoculars in our heavily wooded back yard, and on springtime days to open the door and listen to their songs. I obsessed about the meaning of everything. No need to understand, she insisted, just relax and listen to how beautiful their songs are. I had trouble doing that. Different generations offered such conflicted meanings to *Mockingbird* and mockingbirds' songs. In the wonders of childhood, it is more melody we seek than meaning. Everyone has a right to her own childhood melody. But then we grow up and everything changes.

Our final afternoon together, February 9, 2016, ten days before Nelle's death, was one of the best. Her hearing was good and she was alert and primed for me, wearing her Crimson Tide sweater and strands of Mardi Gras beads we had brought her from New Orleans a year earlier. Two strands were golden. The third featured a hideous green-winged monster labeled "Orpheus" and

"Leviathan." It must have been the ugliest Mardi Gras necklace ever manufactured. Dartie read her our mushy Valentine card. Then I joked that she looked so smashing in her Roll Tide sweater, pedal pushers, Mardi Gras beads, and tennis shoes, that we should depart immediately for New Orleans, only three hours away, where we could eat, drink, and dance naked in the streets. She laughed and laughed and told Dartie once again, "You are married to a nut!" After a moment's reflection, she edited her own sentence, changing "nut" to "maniac." We talked about Truman Capote who was born in New Orleans and might join us in spirit. That inspired another of her chants about Truman in the cemetery: "Here lies . . . and lies, and lies, Truman Capote!"

After her death, I grieved that our final session together had been so silly rather than cerebral. But upon reflecting about what her life had been like after the stroke, I changed my mind. We had a grand time that day being silly. In retrospect, it was an appropriate end.

At 4 a.m. on Friday, February 19, 2016, our phone rang, and Hank Conner told me that Nelle had died in her sleep. She had felt unwell the night before and had died quietly and alone, as she had lived. He told me how relieved he was that I would deliver the eulogy, because he was too distraught by the death of the last of his elders to make it through such an ordeal. I muttered to myself, "Thanks, Hank, I really needed that!"

Unable to go back to sleep and worried how I would manage the funeral service emotionally, I retrieved a copy of the tribute I had delivered at the Birmingham Pledge Foundation award ceremony a decade earlier and began reading it. Midwinter mornings before daylight in Auburn are as quiet as rural graveyards, and I could hear in the distance the mournful whistle and rumble of a train passing through downtown. It reminded me of the iconic dust jacket of the HarperCollins first edition of *Go Set a Watchman*. It also called to mind Nelle's love of trains and, in *Watchman*, Jean Louise's return home to see her father only for the trip to end in lost innocence about him and her uncle. That early morning epiphany made the tears flow.

THE EULOGY I DELIVERED was the one Nelle commanded a decade earlier. It contained nothing about her, only my understanding of her novels' legacy concerning class and racial justice, tolerance for people unlike ourselves, and a shared sense of community.

In light of *Watchman*'s recent publication, I did add two words about her father: "Although imperfect . . ." I assumed any reader of *Mockingbird* and *Watchman* smart enough to come inside during a thunderstorm knew that all people are imperfect and would be neither surprised nor offended by that addition. Not even Nelle. Coley Lee was imperfect. So was his daughter. So are we all.

As Dartie and I packed for the trip to Monroeville, I was of little use, having to answer the phone every few minutes. While talking with Lynn Neering of NPR for the fourth iteration of Nelle's obituary, she interrupted to tell me she had just read a tweet from Jonathan Burnham at HarperCollins, announcing Harper's death to the world: "Rest in peace, Nelle."

That afternoon, some forty family and friends swapped stories in the Prop and Gavel, Tonja's restaurant. Our gathering and the storytelling were typical of Southern wakes, more funny than sad. Outside, the courthouse square filled with mobile television trucks preparing for the following day. Cooperative sheriff's deputies kept the media away from us, and Monroeville citizens were at their best, honoring Nelle's memory by staying home.

Only a few close friends were invited to the memorial service on Saturday afternoon, February 20, at the First United Methodist Church. I presented the eulogy, breathed a sigh of relief, sat down, and grieved as we sang the only hymn Harper had requested, "The King of Love My Shepherd Is."

One of the New York friends had told me that Nelle wanted to be buried in New York City. In her romantic days, Nelle had instructed that a plane should distribute her ashes over Manhattan as had been done for Damon Runyon. In a more reflective mood, Nelle had said she wanted to be buried in one of New York's elite historic cemeteries, either Green-wood in Brooklyn, original site of a Revolutionary War battle, or Woodlawn in Elmira, New York, founded in 1863 for Civil War soldiers, and last resting place for many famous writers, composers, artists, and other celebrities.

Those were not to be. After the memorial service, I trudged down the hill from the church to the adjacent cemetery with Dartie, our son, his wife, and our grandson to the family plot where Nelle was to be buried beside her father, mother, and sister. It seemed an appropriate act of closure.

AN OBITUARY IN *The Economist* the following week described Nelle Harper Lee as a "plain, chubby, chain-smoking Southern girl, living in a cold water flat" while working as an airline clerk and writing a literary classic. The novel published "on the eve of the civil rights era . . . pricked America's conscience," causing reporters to track her down in Monroeville where she nervously smiled at them from the porch of the courthouse "while wishing they would go away."

Francis Bacon wrote an essay in the early seventeenth century in which he advised that "some books are to be tasted, others to be swallowed, and some few to be read only in parts; others to be read but not curiously, and some few to be read wholly and with diligence and attention." When Harold Rabinowitz and Rob Kaplan wrote *A Passion for Books* more than four centuries later, they listed *To Kill a Mockingbird* thirteenth among fifteen American novels which should be "read, wholly, with diligence and attention." I wish Nelle had allowed me discretion to quote that in the eulogy.

The film *Infamous* ends with Harper Lee, portrayed by Sandra Bullock, summarizing the life of her former best friend, Truman Capote, with the inevitable American question: "What next?" As it turned out, the answer was as elusive for Nelle as it was for Truman.

Like naturalist Annie Dillard, I never understood why mockingbirds sing. But like Dartie I finally succumbed to the beauty of their songs. Perhaps singing for the joy of singing is the essence of childhood innocence before a certain age, and adults may never understand why.

ॐ

Coda

IN DECEMBER 2021, SIXTY-ONE YEARS AFTER PUBLICATION OF Harper Lee's first novel, the venerable book review section of the *New York Times* celebrated more than a century of reviews, criticism, and praise. To mark the occasion, editors invited readers from across the globe to select their most beloved book published in the previous one hundred and twenty-five years. Readers from sixty-seven countries responded. Their first choice was a novel written by an essentially one-book author from the most unlikely town in the most unlikely state. Had I been able to break the triumphant news to Nelle, I can recite what would have been her deeply prideful but dismissive response: "All I did was write a book."